Layman's Bible Book Commentary
Philippians, Colossians
1 & 2 Thessalonians
1 & 2 Timothy
Titus, Philemon

LAYMAN'S BIBLE BOOK COMMENTARY

PHILIPPIANS, COLOSSIANS, 1 & 2 THESSALONIANS, 1 & 2 TIMOTHY, TITUS, PHILEMON

VOLUME 22

Malcolm O. Tolbert

BROADMAN PRESS
Nashville, Tennessee

. 4211-92

ISBN: 0-8054-1192-5

Dewey Decimal Classification: 227

Subject heading: BIBLE. N.T. EPISTLES OF PAUL

Library of Congress Catalog Card Number: 79-51998

Printed in the United States of America

Foreword

The *Layman's Bible Book Commentary* in twenty-four volumes was planned as a practical exposition of the whole Bible for lay readers and students. It is based on the conviction that the Bible speaks to every generation of believers but needs occasional reinterpretation in the light of changing language and modern experience. Following the guidance of God's Spirit, the believer finds in it the authoritative word for faith and life.

To meet the needs of lay readers, the *Commentary* is written in a popular style, and each Bible book is clearly outlined to reveal its major emphases. Although the writers are competent scholars and reverent interpreters, they have avoided critical problems and the use of original languages except where they were essential for explaining the text. They recognize the variety of literary forms in the Bible, but they have not followed documentary trails or become preoccupied with literary concerns. Their primary purpose was to show what each Bible book meant for its time and what it says to our own generation.

The Revised Standard Version of the Bible is the basic text of the *Commentary*, but writers were free to use other translations to clarify an occasional passage or sharpen its effect. To provide as much interpretation as possible in such concise books, the Bible text was not printed along with the comment.

Of the twenty-four volumes of the *Commentary*, fourteen deal with Old Testament books and ten with those in the New Testament. The volumes range in pages from 140 to 168. Four major books in the Old Testament and five in the New are treated in one volume each. Others appear in various combinations. Although the allotted space varies, each Bible book is treated as a whole to reveal its basic message with some passages getting special attention. Whatever plan of Bible study the reader may follow, this *Commentary* will be a valuable companion.

Despite the best-seller reputation of the Bible, the average survey of Bible knowledge reveals a good deal of ignorance about it and its primary meaning. Many adult church members seem to think that its study is intended for children and preachers. But some of the newer translations have been making the Bible more readable for all ages. Bible study has branched out from Sunday into other days of the week, and into neighborhoods rather than just in churches. This *Commentary* wants to meet the growing need for insight into all that the Bible has to say about God and his world and about Christ and his fellowship.

BROADMAN PRESS

Contents

PHILIPPIANS

Introduction   13

The Prisoner for Christ (1:1-26)   14
  The Salutation (1:1-2)   14
  The Gratitude of the Prisoner (1:3-7)   15
  The Supplication of the Prisoner (1:8-11)   17
  The Impact of Paul's Imprisonment (1:12-18)   18
  Between Life and Death (1:19-26)   19

Plea for Conduct Worthy of the Gospel (1:27 to 2:18)   20
  Life Worthy of the Gospel (1:27-30)   21
  Resources for Christian Unity (2:1-4)   22
  The Mind of Christ (2:5-11)   23
  The Believers' Appropriate Response (2:12-18)   24

Paul's Plans for the Future (2:19-30)   26
  Plans for Timothy (2:19-24)   26
  Plans for Epaphroditus (2:25-30)   27

The Threat of Jewish Legalism (3:1 to 4:1)   27
  Warning Against the Threat (3:1-3)   27
  Paul's Testimony (3:4-6)   29
  The Righteousness of Faith (3:7-11)   29
  Pressing Toward the Goal (3:12-16)   30
  The Problem of Libertinism (3:17 to 4:1)   31

Exhortations to the Church (4:2-23)   33
  The Problem of Unity (4:2-3)   33
  The Problem of Anxiety (4:4-7)   33
  The Positive Character of Christian Living (4:8-9)   34
  Gratitude for a Gift (4:10-13)   35
  The Philippians' Partnership in the Gospel (4:14-20)   36
  The Conclusion (4:21-23)   37

COLOSSIANS

Introduction   38

The Genuine Gospel (1:1 to 2:5)   39
  The Salutation (1:1-2)   39
  Prayer of Thanksgiving (1:3-5a)   40
  The Fruit of the Gospel (1:5b-8)   41
  Prayer of Intercession (1:9-12)   42
  Deliverance Through the Son (1:13-14)   43
  The All-Sufficient Son (1:15-20)   44
  God's Purpose Seen in the Church (1:21-23)   45
  The Ministry of Paul (1:24-29)   46
  Paul's Desire for the Church (2:1-5)   47

The Colossian Heresy (2:6 to 3:4)   48
  Warning Against Danger (2:6-8)   48
  Fullness in Christ (2:9-15)   49
  The Errors of False Teachings (2:16-23)   51
  The New Life in Christ (3:1-4)   52

The Higher vs. the Lower Life (3:5 to 4:6)   53
  The Old Nature and the New (3:5-11)   53
  The Character of the New Nature (3:12-17)   55
  Family Relationships (3:18 to 4:1)   57
  Prayer and Behavior (4:2-6)   59

Final Greetings (4:7-18)   61
  The Bearers of the Letter (4:7-9)   61
  Messages of Greeting (4:10-15)   62
  Final Instructions (4:16-18)   63

1 THESSALONIANS

Introduction   65

The Reception of the Gospel in Thessalonica (1:1-10)   66
  The Salutation (1:1)   66
  Prayer of Gratitude (1:2-3)   67
  The Success of the Mission in Thessalonica (1:4-7)   68
  The News Spreads (1:8-10)   69

The Work of the Missionaries in Thessalonica (2:1-16)   70
  The Difficulties Confronted (2:1-2)   70
  The Purity of Their Motives (2:3-5)   71
  Gentle as a Nurse (2:6-8)   72
  The Unselfishness of Their Labor (2:9-12)   72
  The Acceptance of the Message (2:13-16)   73

The Mission of Timothy to Thessalonica (2:17 to 3:13)   74
  Paul's Desire to Visit the Church (2:17-20)   74
  The Decision to Send Timothy (3:1-5)   75
  Timothy Returns with Good News (3:6-10)   76
  Paul's Prayer (3:11-13)   77

An Appeal for Godly Living (4:1-12)   77
  Life Pleasing to God (4:1-2)   78
  Holiness in the Sexual Life (4:3-6a)   78
  A Solemn Warning (4:6b-8)   79
  Love for the Brethren (4:9-10)   79
  Conduct in the Community (4:11-12)   80

The Coming of the Lord (4:13 to 5:5)   80
  The Fate of Believers Who Had Died (4:13-18)   80
  The Day of the Lord (5:1-5)   81

Final Admonitions (5:6-28)   82
  Spiritual Alertness Encouraged (5:6-11)   82
  General Exhortations to the Congregation (5:12-28)   83

2 THESSALONIANS

Introduction   85

The Justice of God (1:1-12)   86
  The Salutation (1:1-2)   86
  Paul's Gratitude for the Believers (1:3-4)   86
  Righteous Judgment (1:5-10)   87
  Paul's Prayer for the Thessalonians (1:11-12)   88

The Day of the Lord (2:1-17)   89
  The Problem (2:1-2)   89

The Events of the End Time (2:3-12)   90
Chosen for Salvation (2:13-17)   92

Final Exhortation (3:1-18)   94
Paul's Request for Prayer (3:1-5)   94
The Problem of the Idlers (3:6-15)   95
Concluding Remarks (3:16-18)   96

1 TIMOTHY

Introduction   97

The Salutation (1:1-2)   98

The Threat to the Gospel (1:3-11)   99
The Threat from False Teaching (1:3-6)   99
A Wrong Understanding of the Law (1:7-11)   101

Paul's Praise of God's Grace (1:12-20)   102
For Being Placed in Christ's Service (1:12-14)   102
For Making Him an Example for Other Sinners (1:15-17)   103
The Charge to Timothy (1:18-20)   103

Instructions for the Church (2:1-15)   104
The Scope of Public Prayer (2:1-7)   105
Instructions for Men and Women (2:8-15)   106

The Qualifications of Officers (3:1-13)   108
Bishops (3:1-7)   109
Deacons (3:8-13)   111

The Minister's Task in Difficult Times (3:14 to 4:16)   112
The Truth of the Gospel (3:14-16)   112
False Teachings (4:1-5)   113
The Good Minister (4:6-10)   115
The Example of the Minister (4:11-16)   116

Duties Toward Others (5:1 to 6:2a)   118
Relationships with Various Groups (5:1-2)   118
Responsibilities Toward Widows (5:3-16)   119

Instructions Concerning Elders (5:17-25) 121
Instructions for Slaves (6:1-2*a*) 123

Conclusion (6:2*b*-21) 124
The Motives of the False Teachers (6:2*b*-5) 124
Religion and Money (6:6-10) 125
Charge to Timothy (6:11-16) 126
Further Warning Against Materialism (6:17-19) 127
Final Warning to Timothy (6:20-21) 128

2 TIMOTHY

Introduction 129

Charge to Timothy (1:1 to 2:7) 129
The Salutation (1:1-2) 129
Thanksgiving and Longing (1:3-4) 130
Reminders of the Past (1:5-7) 130
A Partner in Suffering for the Gospel (1:8-10) 131
The Example of Paul's Commitment (1:11-14) 132
A Personal Note (1:15-18) 133
The Good Soldier (2:1-7) 134

The Gospel and Its Enemies (2:8-26) 135
The Heart of the Gospel (2:8-10) 135
A Trustworthy Saying (2:11-13) 136
Handling the Word of Truth (2:14-19) 137
Vessels, Good and Bad (2:20-26) 140

Warning About Impending Dangers (3:1 to 4:5) 142
The Worsening Spiritual Climate (3:1-5) 142
Religious Charlatans (3:6-9) 143
The Lot of the Faithful Minister (3:10-17) 143
Faithfulness to the Word (4:1-5) 145

Paul's Valedictory (4:6-22) 147
The Impending End (4:6-8) 147
Personal Notes (4:9-18) 149
Final Greetings (4:19-22) 150

TITUS

Introduction	152
The Mission of Titus (1:1-16)	153
The Salutation (1:1-4)	153
The Qualifications of Elders (1:5-9)	154
Danger from False Teachers (1:10-16)	155
The Teaching Duties of the Minister (2:1-15)	156
Instructions for Various Groups (2:1-10)	156
The Christian Hope (2:11-15)	158
General Instructions for Christian Living (3:1-15)	159
Christian Conduct in the World (3:1-7)	159
Dealing with Factious Persons (3:8-11)	161
Closing Remarks (3:12-15)	162

PHILEMON

Introduction	164
The Salutation (1-3)	164
Paul's Prayer for Philemon (4-7)	165
An Appeal to Love (8-14)	166
The Conclusion of the Appeal (15-20)	167
Final Remarks (21-25)	168

PHILIPPIANS

Introduction

Philippi, a city in the eastern part of the Roman province of Macedonia, was located on the Egnatian Way, the principal highway from Asia to the West. Philip II of Macedonia, father of Alexander the Great, gave his own name to the city. During the time of the New Testament, it enjoyed the status and privileges of a Roman colony.

Philippi was the first Greek city visited by Paul on his second missionary journey. He was accompanied by Silas (Silvanus) and Timothy (Acts 16:12 ff.). The Philippian church had a close relationship with her apostolic founder. Acts tells of two subsequent visits paid to the region by Paul (Acts 20:1-2,6).

The Occasion of the Letter

When Paul wrote this letter to the church in Philippi, he was in prison. The Philippians had received word of his imprisonment and had sent Epaphroditus with a gift to their beloved apostle. Evidently this was only one of several contributions made to him by the congregation during the course of his ministry (Phil. 4:10-18).

Epaphroditus had become seriously ill after he had reached Paul. News of that illness had greatly disturbed his fellow Christians in Philippi. After he recovered, Paul decided to send him back to the church, knowing that this would bring relief and joy to his friends. Paul took advantage of the opportunity to send a letter to them. In it Paul expressed gratitude to the church for the gift, interpreted the meaning and impact of his imprisonment, communicated his hope of visiting them again, and encouraged them in their Christian living.

Place of Writing

Traditionally people have held that Rome was the place of imprisonment from which Paul wrote Philippians. Acts, of course, tells us about his time in jail in the capital of the empire (Acts 28:14 ff.). The mention of the Praetorium ("praetorian guard"—Phil. 1:13) and Caesar's household (4:22) seems to support this position.

In modern times, however, the traditional view has been questioned. From Philippians itself we learn that Paul was in rather frequent contact with the church during his imprisonment. Some interpreters feel that such close liaison between Paul and the church would have been difficult, if not impossible, were he as far away as Rome. Caesarea and Ephesus have been suggested as likely places for the writing of the imprisonment epistles.

By way of conclusion we may say that Philippians could have been written from some other place. However, it seems best to adopt the traditional position that it was written from Rome. We would date the epistle, therefore, about AD 63.

The Prisoner for Christ

1:1-26

The Salutation (1:1-2)

As was his custom, Paul began the letter to the Philippians according to the pattern usually followed in first-century letter writing. The pattern consisted of these elements: (1) the name of the writer, (2) the name(s) of the recipient(s), (3) a greeting, and (4) a prayer for the recipient(s). His custom, however, was to enlarge upon these conventional elements in significant ways. For example, usually Paul did not give just his name and the names of the recipients. He added meaningful comments about himself and about them.

Timothy is associated with Paul in the salutation of the letter, but we gather from the content that Paul is solely responsible for it. Timothy was at Paul's side during his imprisonment. He, along with Silas, had participated in the original mission to Philippi (Acts 16:1 ff.). It was natural, therefore, for Paul to include Timothy in his greeting to the Philippians. He called Timothy and himself "servants of Christ Jesus." The word is literally "slaves."

Paul probably used "servants" to emphasize his absolute commitment to Jesus Christ. He and Timothy were slaves: Jesus Christ was their Master or Lord. Paul's complete submission to Jesus Christ is certainly prominent in this letter.

The letter is addressed "To all the saints . . . at Philippi." *Saints* is a word used for God's people. They are not holy because of their own moral achievement. But they are all saints because they belong to God. Anything or anybody that belongs to God can be called holy.

Paul singled out bishops and deacons for special mention in his salutation. *Bishops* means overseers and probably refers to the members of the church who had special administrative responsibilities. The word *deacons* means waiters or helpers and may refer to members who assisted the bishops in performing their responsibilities.

This reference to bishops and deacons is unusual in Paul's greeting. It may be explained by the fact that Paul was writing to thank the church for an offering sent to him. Bishops and deacons could designate the people responsible in the church for raising such offerings. We should note that there were several bishops, as well as deacons, in the church in Philippi. Our knowledge of the organizational forms followed by churches in the New Testament period is limited and sketchy. We have no way of knowing how the church in Philippi actually functioned.

The characteristic greeting in Paul's letters brings together two great words. "Grace" is God's undeserved favor toward us, manifested particularly in the giving of his Son. The usual Jewish greeting was *shalom* or *peace*. For Paul the word described the new relationship between God and the believer and among believers themselves. Since grace and peace come from "God" through "Jesus Christ," both the "Father" and the Son can be named as their source.

The Gratitude of the Prisoner (1:3-7)

Imprisoned and separated from the believers in Philippi as he was, Paul could do one thing for his beloved friends. He could pray for them. He believed with all his heart that his prayers were both necessary and helpful to other believers.

Several characteristics of Paul's prayers for the Philippian Christians emerge from his remarks. They were prayers of thanksgiving. When Paul saw good things in the lives of Christians, he thanked God for those good things, for he recognized the Father as the source of every Christian grace. Moreover, he remembered and prayed for all the believers. This emphasis upon the whole church is characteristic of Philippians in particular (e.g., 1:1) and of Paul's letters in general.

The apostle's prayers were characterized also by *joy*. This is a key word in the letter—all the more remarkable when we remember that Paul was in prison.

The word for prayer (v. 4) is used of a special kind of prayer. It is petition or supplication. Paul was saying, therefore, that every time he went to God to make supplication for the Philippian believers he never failed to thank God for them.

The reason for the thanksgiving and joy is stated in concrete, specific terms. It was the Philippians' "partnership in the gospel" (v. 5). *Partnership* translates *koinonia,* one of the great words in Paul's Christian vocabulary. Many times we can also understand it as "fellowship." The Christian life is a partnership or fellowship. It is a shared life. We share with all other believers the blessings of God's grace. We also share with them the responsibilities of our new life in the proclamation of the gospel. If the gospel is to reach our world, an effective partnership among many people is necessary. Some must give, stay, witness, and pray, as the Philippians had done. Some must receive, go, witness, and pray, as Paul had done.

Paul was supremely sure that the faithful, loving service so characteristic of the Philippians would continue and grow in the future. After all, it was God who had begun "a good work" in the Philippians. He could be trusted to continue it and to "bring it to completion at the day of Jesus Christ." This is the day of Christ's appearing, the final consummation of history, and the complete victory of God's rule.

Verse 7 seems to be a justification of Paul's special feeling for the Philippians. "I hold you in my heart" may also be translated in the opposite way: "You hold me in your heart" (see NEB). Indeed, it makes more sense in the context. Paul's attitude toward his readers is "right" because of the special place they have given him in their affection.

Moreover, they were "partakers" with Paul of "grace." Partakers, a cognate of the word for partnership (v. 5), can also be translated partners or, literally, "fellow sharers." The word "grace" is somewhat surprising, since it is related to Paul's "imprisonment." We might expect to find the word *suffering* instead. Suffering, however, if it were in connection with his proclamation of the gospel, was an undeserved privilege which was granted to him by the grace of God. Later in the letter Paul spoke about the privilege of sharing in the suffering of Christ (3:10).

The Philippians would not allow the apostle to go unnoticed or forgotten in this time of his great trial. They had sent him a gift as a concrete expression of their fellowship with him in his imprisonment.

"Defense" referred to the plea made by the prisoner before the court. "Confirmation" denoted the evidence presented to validate the defense. From Paul's statement, however, we see that he was not attempting to defend or exonerate himself. He used the opportunity of the trial to press the claims of the gospel.

The Supplication of the Prisoner (1:8-11)

Paul occasionally used the phrase "God is my witness" when he wanted to make an especially solemn declaration. God is the highest witness to the truth, for only he knows the heart. Paul spoke so solemnly because he wanted his readers to be absolutely certain of his longing to see them. *Yearning* is our feeling when we are separated from those we love.

The love that made Paul "yearn" for his brothers and sisters was no less than the "affection of Christ Jesus" himself, a bold declaration. Paul knew, however, that his love for the Philippians came from the Lord. He regarded love for other members of God's family as the primary expression of the new life in Christ (1 Cor. 13). "Affection" is literally the viscera, the heart, lungs, liver, and kidneys (KJV—bowels). They were regarded by the Greeks as the seat of affection.

After assuring his readers of his love for them, Paul moved naturally to the petition that their "love" for one another might increase in an overflowing manner. This word for love (v. 9) is *agape,* the one generally used in the New Testament for God's kind of love. Therefore, Paul prayed that the love of the believers might be accompanied by "knowledge and all discernment." This knowledge is always knowledge of God or of the things of God. Discernment translates a word which denotes the capacity to make moral distinctions and ethical decisions.

The need for this capacity is seen in the clause "so that you may approve what is excellent." The translation of the NIV probably gives the sense of the clause somewhat more clearly: "so that you may be able to discern what is best." Believers need to be able to distinguish not only between the good and bad but also between the good and best.

The end result is also mentioned by Paul. We shall be "pure and blameless for the day of Christ." The best life which we can present to the Lord will be one that is lived by the power and under the direction of his love.

Paul did not express his hope for his readers in a negative way only. Being a Christian is much more than being "blameless." Paul wanted them to be "filled with the fruits of righteousness." Righteousness, therefore, is more than being justified or declared right before God. It is a dynamic force, working in the believer to produce a harvest of good fruit. From Paul's point of view, the day of the harvest will be the "day of Christ."

Christians will not be able to take credit for their accomplishments. The harvest is produced by God's righteousness working "through Jesus Christ." It does not reflect on the believer so that he is praised. Rather, it leads to the "glory and praise of God."

The Impact of Paul's Imprisonment (1:12-18)

"I want you to know" translates a phrase usually employed by Paul to call attention to his point. The point was exactly this: Whatever his personal problems might have been, they served to advance the gospel. That was what mattered to Paul; it is also what should matter to his readers, although we could wish that Paul had given us more information about his personal situation.

The gospel has been advanced in two ways. First, some people have heard the gospel who needed to hear it. "Praetorian guard" is literally "Praetorium." Originally the word meant the tent or headquarters of a Roman general. It was also used for the residence or palace of a governor.

People who place Paul's imprisonment in Rome believe that the word referred to the imperial guards who had heard the gospel because Paul was their prisoner. They understood that his imprisonment was in "Christ"—that is, resulting from Paul's service to the one he called Lord.

Second, some people had begun to preach the gospel who needed to preach it. Paul declared that "most of the brethren" had been encouraged to give a bold witness to their faith. Often the example of a faithful witness to the gospel has the effect of inspiring others to be more courageous than they might have been.

Unfortunately, the situation in the Roman church was not altogether ideal. Paul had his enemies also among the church members. The situation is certainly not made clear by his remarks. We gather, however, that there were "jealous and quarrelsome" people, motivated by the "spirit of selfish ambition" (TEV) who used the gospel to promote their own position in the church. They attempted to undermine

Paul's influence and leadership among other believers. Perhaps they pointed to his imprisonment as an evidence of failure rather than success.

Other people, however, preached Christ "from good will." They were positive in that their only concern was to lead others to know Christ and to build up the fellowship. They understood the real purpose of Paul's imprisonment. He had been placed there for the "defense of the gospel"—that is, to present its claims.

In no passage does Paul rise to greater heights than in this one. Hurt? He must have been. To be misunderstood by his brothers was a source of greater pain than the hatred of the gospel's enemies. Yet Paul rose above whatever competition and maneuvering he detected in the church.

Between Life and Death (1:19-26)

"This will turn out for my deliverance" presents difficulties for the interpreter. "Deliverance" translates the word usually rendered as "salvation" in the New Testament. Often the word meant deliverance from peril, and most versions take it in that sense. The problem is, however, that Paul did not seem so confident of being set free from his imprisonment in his other comments. The clause is a quotation from the Greek Old Testament version of Job 13:16. In it Job affirmed in the midst of his suffering that he would be vindicated. This may be the key to understanding what Paul meant. He meant it in the same way that Job did. Whatever happened, his God would vindicate him. The judgment of the Roman court was really irrelevant in the light of this confidence.

Paul's confidence was buoyed by support from two sources—the "prayers" of his friends and the "help of the Spirit of Jesus Christ." The Lord himself promised that the Spirit would aid his followers in times of persecution (Matt. 10:19-20).

Paul's exclusive concern in the midst of his affliction was that he "not be at all ashamed." In the New Testament "to be ashamed" may describe cowardice in the face of persecution which can result in a denial of the Lord. Whatever happens to him in the future, Paul's "eager expectation and hope" is that he will be faithful. If he only remains true to Christ, the Lord will be "honored" in his "body" whether he lives or dies. For Paul "body" meant the person.

Verse 21 does not contrast life and death. Paul meant that as long as he lived he would live for Christ. In that way Christ would be honored. If living for Christ resulted in his death, that was no tragedy. The faithful follower of Jesus Christ does not lose when he dies. To the contrary, he gains. Paul was concerned that the Philippians have a Christian view of his own death, should that occur. Rather than being saddened, they should rejoice over his gain should he be executed.

Given his view of life and death, Paul found it difficult to make a choice. The reason for that difficulty becomes clear. If he had no one to think about other than himself, he would prefer to die in order to "be with Christ." He would then be able to enjoy that full fellowship of which his present experience was only a tantalizing foretaste.

But he did not have only himself to think about. He had to consider his Philippian friends. He knew that they needed him. His gain would be their loss. Love dictated, therefore, that he place their needs above his own desires.

Apparently Paul thought that the possibility for his exoneration and release was good. This would enable him to fulfill his yearning to see the Philippians again. A visit to them would serve two purposes—their "progress and joy in the faith."

Clearly a special relationship existed between the Philippian church and the great apostle. They took tremendous pride in him. Aware that his return to them would be an occasion for the expression of that pride, the apostle reminded his friends that they should "glory in Christ Jesus."

Plea for Conduct Worthy of the Gospel
1:27 to 2:18

Aware that he might be prevented by circumstances from returning to Philippi, Paul used this letter to present to them the appeal of his heart. From this appeal we can perceive the area in which Paul believed they could make progress in the faith.

Life Worthy of the Gospel (1:27-30)

Paul's appeal was for conduct worthy of the gospel. Believers are to "stand firm." This verb is used to describe that which is stable and lasting. The powers of evil assault the community in order to bring about its collapse and fall. The church is to firmly resist all such assaults.

Believers are to stand firm "in one spirit." It is difficult to determine if "spirit" here is the human spirit (as understood in the RSV) or the Holy Spirit. The Spirit of God is the source of the unity of the church. He transforms believers so that they are united in their own spirits. Perhaps Paul was thinking of both.

Whatever the case, the appeal is for unity. When believers live worthily of the gospel, there is unity in the church. Paul went on to stress the importance of unity by adding the phrase "with one mind." They are not to go off in different directions. They are one in their allegiance to the Lord, one in their understanding of the priorities of the Christian life, one in their purposes and goals.

Paul viewed the Christian life as a struggle. But Christians struggled "side by side." What they are contending for is the "faith of the gospel." Faith is not dogmatic or propositional truth. Faith means trust in the Lord. The attack of the world is directed toward destroying that faith.

Fearlessness is to be characteristic of Christians as they face the assault of their enemies. The courage that Paul spoke about is not self-generated. It comes "from God"; it is his gift to his people. As such it is an "omen." God is on the side of his people, and he demonstrates it by giving them courage. This means that their enemies are going to lose. It also means that the church is going to win. "Salvation" here refers to the ultimate deliverance of God's people from all hostile and evil powers. Paul normally used the term in that sense.

One of the striking aspects of Paul's view of suffering is the positive way that he interpreted it. The verb "has been granted" is a cognate of the word for grace. It means something that God has given as a favor. To suffer for Christ, therefore, is a privilege granted by God. The privilege of believing and of suffering are given together. Paul could not conceive of a genuine Christian commitment that did not involve hardship.

The privilege of suffering is defined by the phrase "for his sake." To have the opportunity of making some sacrifice for the one who did so much for us can be nothing less than an expression of grace. To be able to do nothing for him who died for us—that would be a deprivation.

The Philippians also had the encouragement of Paul's own example. When he had been with them, they had seen how he had resolutely faced opposition to the gospel. They had also received reports about the situation in which Paul found himself at the moment. Christians in whatever place are united in the "same conflict." This, too, is an expression of their oneness in Christ.

Resources for Christian Unity (2:1-4)

One of the aspects of Paul's theology that many Christians fail to appreciate is his view of the church. God's purpose in Christ is to create a community, bound together in a common life, characterized by mutual love and encouragement. Such is the view of the church which Paul expressed in this passage.

"In Christ" often is a practical synonym for the church in Paul's writings. One version brings out the idea more clearly by rendering the phrase "from being united with Christ" (NIV). From the apostle's point of view resources of "encouragement" and "love" are present in the Christian community. All Christians share the benefits given by the "Spirit" of God who creates the fellowship of the church. To have the Spirit is to have "affection and sympathy" for fellow believers. God wants to create a community in which the resources are available to help us in temptation, trial, and discouragement.

"Joy" is one of the keynotes of the epistle to the Philippians. Paul had already expressed the joy that he had received from them. But that joy could be even fuller as the unity of the church became greater and greater.

The church is to be one in purpose ("mind") and one in love. That is the positive side. But there is also a negative side. There are dangers to be avoided. These dangers are twofold. First, there is the problem of "selfishness." This word means "party spirit." The church is always in danger of being split into competing groups or parties.

Second, there is the danger of "conceit." Pride or vanity destroys unity. Pride makes a person put himself at the center of things. When this happens in the church, it becomes full of competing centers, each one promoting himself or, as Paul put it, "his own interests."

"Humility," not pride, is the hallmark of the Christian. Humility is not weakness but strength. If we have a poor self-image and let people run over us, that is weakness. If we are strong enough, however, to choose to commit ourselves to the welfare of others, this is a virtue. Paul illustrated this truth vividly, as we see in the next passage.

The Mind of Christ (2:5-11)

When Paul spoke about the mind and spirit which should characterize the Christian community, his meaning was determined by the reality of that mind encountered in Jesus Christ. The "mind"—that is, the attitude or disposition expressed in the incarnation of God's Son—is to govern the Christian in his relationship with other believers. Paul was speaking about relationships among believers rather than the attitude within the individual.

Interpreters agree generally that 2:6-11 was a Christian hymn used in the worship of the church and inserted by Paul into the letter at this point. Paul probably did not compose it, but it expressed precisely the idea which he wanted to emphasize.

The hymn reminded the readers of the glory of Christ prior to the incarnation. He was in the "form of God." The reader of the English text could misunderstand the word "form" and take it to mean that Jesus was like God. This misses the idea in the word altogether. "Form" denotes the expression of the reality itself. The form of God is synonymous with the glory of God. Paul asserted that Christ was really God and that his glory was the glory of God.

But Christ did not "count equality with God a thing to be grasped." Perhaps Paul had in mind a contrast between the two Adams. The first Adam attempted to seize equality with God (Gen. 3:5). The second Adam, Christ, possessed that glory as his own, but he did not hold on to it. He exchanged the form of God for the opposite, "taking the form of a servant" or, literally, "of a slave." He was Lord, possessing supreme authority. He became a slave, one who can only obey.

The emphasis is upon the free, voluntary action of Christ. Any view of the incarnation and the cross must respect this idea. What Jesus did, he did willingly. The cross was not what God did to Jesus. It was what Jesus as God freely chose.

When Paul used the phrases "form of a servant" and "likeness of men," he did not mean that Jesus was like a man merely in appearance. He was genuinely human in every respect, not only in outward form but also in feelings, thoughts, and vulnerability. But he was also different from all other men. That difference is seen in the perfection of his obedience. He did what man was originally created to do; he lived by the will of God. This is emphasized by the term "slave" and by the assertion that he "became obedient unto death." Unlike the first Adam, he did not assert his autonomy in rebellion against God.

The extent of his obedience is defined by the words "unto death." Death marks the limits, the ultimate boundary of obedience. Jesus was willing to do what God wanted even though it meant death for him. And this was no ordinary death. It was humiliating, shameful, inglorious execution as a criminal—"even death on a cross."

The way to glory is the way of the cross—for Christ and for his followers. Christ was the actor in the first part of the hymn. God becomes the actor in the second part. No one achieves glory by seeking it for himself. Glory is given by God to the one who does not seek it. Seeking one's own glory ends in disaster, as it did for the first Adam. Seeking the welfare of others leads to glory, as it did for the second Adam (Christ).

The one who was humiliated by men was "exalted" by God. Because of his matchless obedience, God gave him a matchless "name." That name, of course, is Lord. In order to speak about Christ's unparalleled lordship, Paul picked up phrases from Isaiah 45:23. The recognition of his lordship will be universal. "Every knee" shall bow before this sovereign Lord; "every tongue" shall "confess"—that is, acknowledge—him to be Lord. His authority will encompass the whole created order "in heaven and on earth and under the earth." The end result of the universal dominion of Christ will be that God will receive the "glory" due him.

The Believers' Appropriate Response (2:12-18)

People who have the mind of Christ will be characterized by obedience, even as he was. Since obedience was above all to God, the apostle's absence should not affect the life of the church. Indeed, the community should respond with an even greater degree of responsibility.

"Salvation" is used in the usual Pauline sense of the goal of the Christian life. Paul did not mean at all that Christians were responsible for saving themselves. They were responsible for living out the meaning of their salvation, for moving toward that goal in obedient and loving commitment to their Lord. "Work out your own salvation" means simply "Be faithful in living the Christian life." "Your own salvation" expresses the fact that the Philippians were on their own in the sense that they were without the resources of wisdom and support that Paul had provided while with them. It does not mean that they were without God's presence. Paul himself wrote: "God is at work in you."

Their attitude was to be one of "fear and trembling." This means that they were not to be arrogant and self-righteous. One of the constant dangers facing Christians who are trying to live the Christian life is pride. Paul admonished Christians to work. But he reminded them that they were not to take credit for their achievements. The Christian life is the work of God. From him comes the will to follow Christ in obedience. From him comes the energy to fulfill our commitment. His is the purpose toward which we work. "For his good pleasure" can also be translated "for his own chosen purpose" (NEB).

The attitude with which the believer serves Christ is also important. "Grumbling" and "questioning" are unworthy of Christ's servants. If believers are loyal to their Lord, they too will experience rejection, persecution, and hardship. They are to meet all of this with dauntless faith and undiminished joy.

When there is a coherence between actions and attitudes—that is, when obedience is accompanied by joy and thankfulness—Christ's followers are "blameless and innocent." They are truly children of God, linked to him in love and faithfulness, and "without blemish."

Such Christians stand in stark contrast to the unbelieving world. They live "in the midst of a crooked and perverse generation." Unbelievers are perverse in that they are always turning away from God to evil.

Among such people, Christians are to "shine as lights in the world." "Lights" probably refers to the heavenly bodies or stars that illuminate a dark sky Paul's view of the unbelieving world was a dark world, without the light of the knowledge of God. The Christians' responsibility is thus seen in clear terms. They are to "shine like stars in a dark world" (NEB).

They are responsible for "holding fast the word of life." This is the good news of God's redemption through Jesus Christ. Christians are to resist the pressures that would force them to turn away from the one message needed by a dark world.

Paul felt the success of his own life was intertwined with the commitment of his Philippian brothers. The "day of Christ" refers to the day of the Lord's return. Paul hoped that on that day the Philippians would be able to meet their Lord with a record of faithful service.

Apparently Paul had come to believe that he might not be alive at the return of Christ. There was a good possibility that he would be executed. But even that is seen in a positive light. The background for Paul's metaphor (v. 17) is Jewish sacrificial practice. In connection with the burnt offering, a drink offering was poured out upon the altar. This gave Paul a means of relating his death to the lives of the Philippians. Their "faith" was the "offering" which they proffered to God. The shedding of his blood was an act of worship. It would be "poured" as a drink offering on the altar. The authorities might think they had taken Paul's life. Unwittingly they would be serving as priests at God's altar. They could not take Paul's life, for he had previously offered it up to God.

Paul's Plans for the Future

2:19-30

Plans for Timothy (2:19-24)

Although he lacked the freedom at the moment to travel to Philippi, Paul planned to renew his contact with his friends. If all went well, he would send Timothy as his personal messenger to them in order that he might receive "news" from the church. That plan was subject to change. Paul could only speak in terms of a "hope" because he did not know whether he would be alive to carry it out. It was his hope "in the Lord." All that Paul did was "in the Lord," in keeping with his commitment to the Lord and the Lord's will for his life.

"Like" (v. 20) is a weak translation of an expressive word which literally means "equal souled." "He is the only one who shares my feelings" (TEV) is far better. Paul's meaning is illuminated by the comment: "who will be genuinely anxious for your welfare." Others were available, we gather, whom Paul did not want to send. They did not have the proper attitude, for they used the gospel and churches to promote "their own interests." Timothy's concern was solely for the "welfare" of the church—the distinguishing mark of the good minister.

The Philippians themselves knew Timothy's "worth." This translates a term which means "worth proven through testing." Timothy had proven his worth in Philippi where he had served "in the gospel" with Paul "as a son with a father."

The delay in sending Timothy is explained. Paul wanted to wait until Timothy could carry news about the outcome of his trial. If Paul were freed, he would visit the church himself soon thereafter.

Plans for Epaphroditus (2:25-30)

Epaphroditus had been chosen by the Philippian church to bear their gift to Paul. As a result of this mission in which he had risked his life, Epaphroditus had become gravely ill. News of his serious condition had been received by the Philippians, causing them great distress. Epaphroditus had heard of their concern and was himself distressed by it. Because of his "longing" to see his friends, Paul had decided to send Epaphroditus back to Philippi. We assume that he carried this letter to the church.

The knowledge that the Philippians would "rejoice at seeing him again" would also cause Paul to "be less anxious." Anything that brought sorrow to his beloved church also caused distress for their apostle.

The Threat of Jewish Legalism

3:1 to 4:1

Warning Against the Threat (3:1-3)

Apparently Paul was about to bring his letter to a close in verse 1. The word translated "finally" ("In conclusion"—TEV) indicates this. "Rejoice" can also mean "farewell" (NEB) in classical Greek. Then there is the abrupt change in tone from the rest of the letter, beginning with verse 2. Suddenly Paul became harsh and vociferous, whereas the rest of the letter is characterized by love, gratitude, and understanding, even where Paul addressed himself to problems in the church. Also, there has been no hint up to this point that the problem of Jewish legalism was a threat to the church.

This has led some scholars to suppose that the polemical passage in chapter 3 is part of another letter written by Paul. Such a view is possibly correct. However, there is no concrete evidence to support it. Moreover, Paul's comment in verse 1 to the effect that he did not find it "irksome" to repeat himself most logically points to what follows. No doubt Paul had warned the Philippians previously against the possibility of Jewish legalism, for this was a constant problem in the churches. It is difficult to find anything in the preceding portion of the letter to which the remark might apply. Probably something happened while Paul was in the process of writing the letter to trigger the outburst against Jewish legalism.

We may assume that the danger against which Paul issued such an emphatic warning came from outside the church rather than from within. It seems that traveling representatives of the "circumcision party" made it a practice to visit Paul's churches in their effort to get Gentile believers to adopt Jewish practices.

Paul described those representatives in the harshest of terms. He repeated his warning three times. Dog was sometimes used in Jewish circles as a crude designation for Gentiles. Perhaps Paul was simply turning their own terminology against the dangerous teachers.

The apostle called them "evil-workers." He also described them as "those who mutilate the flesh." In Greek this is a play on words. Mutilation is similar to circumcision. The legalists called what they did circumcision. They believed that being circumcised meant they belonged to God. Paul said that such a practice is mutilation, a useless cutting of the flesh.

Circumcision at best was but a symbol of an inward reality. Paul was not opposed to circumcision among Jews. But from his point of view, those who elevated the symbol to a place of first importance and put their trust in it did not belong to the people of God. To require circumcision of Gentiles as a prerequisite to their acceptance by the church was inalterably opposed by Paul. The "true circumcision," or the genuine people of God, were those who possessed the inward reality.

Paul mentioned three characteristics of God's covenant people. They "worship God in spirit." Spiritual worship is inward, antithetical to the external fleshly ritual of those who think they please God by submitting to circumcision. In essence this leads to self-worship. God's people "glory in Christ" rather than boasting about their own superiority. The other side of this is that they put no "confidence in the flesh."

The confidence of the people who exalted circumcision was based on a physical rite. Genuine believers do not trust in any physical distinctions or in their own achievements. Their trust is in a God of power and glory who redeems them through Jesus Christ.

Paul's Testimony (3:4-6)

Paul could match all the claims of the self-righteous legalists. Indeed, his situation when measured by fleshly standards was superior to theirs. First, there was the matter of his heritage. He was an Israelite by birth, "circumcised" as an infant "on the eighth day" according to the traditions of his people. This means that he was not a proselyte to Judaism.

Not only so, but he was of the "tribe of Benjamin," second only to Judah in honor. He was a "Hebrew born of Hebrews." This means that his parents spoke the native dialect, Aramaic, unlike many of the Jews living in foreign areas who could not speak the language of their people. Paul himself was fluent in the language (Acts 22:2). Ritually, racially, and culturally, therefore, Paul's claims to purity were unsurpassed.

Second, there was the matter of his own moral achievements. He belonged to the sect of the Pharisees, recognized by the Jewish people as superior in their devotion to a life governed by the "law." He was so zealous in his defense of Judaism that he had persecuted the church, which he had perceived as a threat to his way of life. Finally, measured by the standards of the law as interpreted by the Pharisees, his "righteousness" was above approach.

The Righteousness of Faith (3:7-11)

When he was confronted by Christ, however, Paul came to see that he had to make a fundamental and radical decision. He could hold on to those advantages of birth and moral achievement that he possessed. Or he could trust Christ for salvation. He could not do both. He had to make a choice.

Paul, therefore, made his choice. He would give up his personal advantages "for the sake of Christ." One could not know Christ as long as he did not make him the only reality and value of his life. Paul came to view everything else as "loss," as having no value at all. Nothing else was worth his love, his time, his devotion. In comparison to Christ everything else was "so much garbage" (NEB). The word also was a common term for excrement ("dung"—KJV). Paul's statement must have been shocking to Jews. He called what they held dear "garbage" or "excrement."

It is only when Christ becomes the sole, supreme purpose of the life that we can "gain Christ." Believers in Christ have a righteousness that comes "from God" and not from their own achievement. This "in Christ" position cannot be gained by human endeavor. It is possible only "through faith." Faith is the radical commitment of life to Christ and to him alone as the only hope of a relationship with God.

"Righteousness" is primarily a matter of relationship. The righteous man is by definition the one who is in a right relationship with God. We cannot earn this relationship by our own righteousness. But what we cannot earn, God freely gives us by grace through faith.

To "know" Christ is to be in an intimate relationship with him through faith. The person who knows Christ experiences the "power of his resurrection." The supreme manifestation of God's power was the resurrection of Jesus from the dead. This is the power that is given to the Christian.

But there is another mark of the person who knows Christ. He shares in the "sufferings" of his Lord. Christ in his incarnation had not exhausted the necessity for suffering. He still suffered through his persecuted body, the church. In Paul's mind his own suffering as a preacher of the gospel was lifted to the highest possible level. Through it he had a special kind of fellowship with Christ through sharing in the suffering of his Lord (see Col. 1:24).

"Becoming like him in his death" points the reader back to Paul's description of Christ in 2:6-11. The Christian is to follow the example of Jesus Christ in obedience to death.

Beyond all this, however, there is the Christian hope. The believer knows the power which operates in Christ now. He also shares in Christ's sufferings now. He may die for Christ, as Paul was to do. He also has the confident hope, however, that his future will be the same as his Lord's. Like Christ and in relationship with him, the believer expects to "attain the resurrection from the dead."

Pressing Toward the Goal (3:12-16)

Paul wanted to guard against any misunderstanding of his previous comments. He wanted the readers to know that he had not crossed the finish line in the Christian race as yet.

Paul wanted the Philippians to know that he had not achieved perfection. "Christ once took hold of me" (NEB). Of that he was sure. But he had not reached the goal of life that had become a glorious possibility when Christ had seized him. He did believe that he would obtain the glorious inheritance which lay before him.

In order to explain what he meant, Paul used the illustration of the athletic games. He was like a runner in a race. In races the winner's prize, the laurel wreath of the victor, was often placed at the finish line as an added incentive to the contestants.

Like the runners in a race, his attention was totally focused on the prize at the end. His concentration was complete. He did not glance back, for to do so could mean the loss of stride and speed. So he forgot what lay behind in order to "press on toward the goal." The prize was the crown of eternal life toward which God had called him "in Christ Jesus."

The apostle called on the "mature" to take the same approach to their Christian life. *Mature* is the adjectival form of the verb translated "am perfect" in verse 12. Paul's theology is totally against a concept of "sinless perfection" or "super spirituality." The only kind of maturity possible to us is the recognition that we are not yet perfect and the commitment of our lives to running the race to the end.

Paul had a concluding injunction about this matter to his readers. He knew that their knowledge was imperfect and their progress incomplete. He did not expect them to be perfect. But they did have the responsibility to "hold true to what we have attained." As the NEB translates it, "Only let our conduct be consistent with the level we have already reached" (v. 16). There is always the possibility that the immature believer, confused by the exaggerated claims of a shortcut to a better and more perfect way, will forsake what he has already attained. It happens all the time.

The Problem of Libertinism (3:17 to 4:1)

From the very beginning believers in the gospel of grace have had to walk the thin edge between legalism, on the one hand, and libertinism, on the other. Paul dealt in the preceding verses with the problem of legalism. Now he turned his attention to the opposite problem.

Libertinism is used to describe the view of people who believed that the gospel of grace relieved them of all responsibility for living a moral life. Since they are saved by grace, it does not matter how much they sin. Paul's remarks show how widespread and serious the problem was. He had found it necessary to talk about this many times to the Philippians. Even now he wrote with "tears" in his eyes. These were tears of grief over the damage that was being done to the Christian cause by immoral people.

Paul did not mince words. They were "enemies of the cross of Christ." Paul believed that in the cross of Christ we are crucified to the world. There is complete discontinuity between the old life and the new. A radical change takes place both in our values and in our goals. To Paul, when a person said that he had been redeemed through the death of Christ but continued to live according to the patterns of the old life, that was a contradiction. Such people were actually in opposition to the very thing for which Christ died.

The destiny of these immoral people, according to Paul, is not eternal life but "destruction." Their life was not determined by the will of Christ but by their own unredeemed desires. Therefore, their "god [was] the belly" ("appetite" in NEB).

Paul said: "They glory in their shame." This probably reflects libertine theology. There were people who said that the more they sinned, the greater was their witness to the grace of God. Instead of being ashamed of their sin, they were proud of it. In contrast to those who pursued the upward call, their "minds" were "set on earthly things."

Genuine believers are different. They are not citizens of this world, but they belong to a heavenly "commonwealth." They are not satisfied with earthly pleasures, possessions, or achievements. Their lives are lived in the daily expectation of their coming Lord. They know that their present mode of existence is a temporary, passing one. They look forward to a transformation which will change this "lowly body" into a "glorious body," which will be like his. They are confident that they will not be disappointed. Their transformation is guaranteed by an unlimited, universal "power which enables [Christ] to subject all things to himself."

In the light of their future hope, believers are to "stand firm thus in the Lord" (4:1). Notice how Paul united the appeal for responsible Christian living to a reminder of our dependence on the Lord. We are responsible for resisting the attacks of the enemy upon our faith and commitment. But we can only stand firm because we are "in the Lord."

Exhortations to the Church
4:2-23

The Problem of Unity (4:2-3)

One of the noblest passages in Paul's writings is the appeal to unity found in chapter 1. Now we find that this appeal was motivated, at least in part, by actual problems of disunity in the church. Two women, Euodia and Syntyche, were at odds with one another. We know nothing further about these women. We are not told the reason for their quarrel. From what Paul said, they were Christian women who had a distinguished record of service in the gospel. This is an illustration of how dedicated Christians can have problems in relationships and thus contradict the work of God's grace in their lives.

We do not know the identity of the man addressed as Paul's "true yokefellow." Evidently he was one of the church's leaders. Paul appealed to him for "help" in reconciling the two women. This appeal underlines our responsibility for maintaining the fellowship of the body when there are problems between other Christians.

Clement, mentioned here, is also unknown otherwise. We could assume that he and other fellow workers had died. This is a possible implication of the affirmation that their "names are in the book of life."

The Problem of Anxiety (4:4-7)

The verb "rejoice" may also be translated "farewell." It was commonly used as a closing greeting in letters of the day. Joy is one of the keynotes of this epistle. Even when the circumstances of life are adverse, the believer can "rejoice in the Lord." The presence of Christ, the meaning that he gives to life, and the hope which he inspires are all reasons for rejoicing. Paul could say rejoice "always" because the reasons for Christian joy are not affected by the present situation in which we find ourselves.

The word translated "forbearance" has a variety of possible meanings, as we can see in the versions. Gentleness or kindness in relation to others is a central idea. This forbearance or gentleness is to be manifested to "all," both pagans and Christians.

"The Lord is at hand" expresses the confident expectation of early Christians. Their lives were oriented toward the future whose major event was the coming of their Lord. Paul had the conviction that the Lord was near and could appear at any moment. Many contemporary Christians are much the poorer because they do not have the sense of the nearness of the Lord.

"Anxiety" is a contradiction of the life of faith. It is the destructive, self-defeating worry about whether our needs are going to be met. It expresses itself in the idolatry of things.

We do have needs. Rather than worrying about them, however, the Christian approach is to make those needs known through "requests to God." The cure for anxiety is confident trust in a loving heavenly Father whose provision for our welfare far exceeds our poor power to ask or think.

The result of such trust is the "peace of God." Peace is one way to describe salvation. There is no longer any hostility between the redeemed person and his God. But Paul here must have been thinking about the fruit of this new relationship. When we trust in God to supply our needs, that peace or serenity which is beyond our power to understand or describe becomes the condition in which we live. "Hearts" and "minds" are generally synonymous terms in the Bible. Anxiety causes us to have divided loyalties and divided, warring, and conflicting thoughts. God's peace brings a resolution of these conflicts. His "peace" keeps our "hearts and minds."

The Positive Character of Christian Living (4:8-9)

"Finally" is found again here (see 3:1). Paul may have been thinking about bringing the letter to a close, although we know there is still more. The word may represent, however, merely a shift in thought.

The list of eight virtues is similar to those found in non-Christian Greek thought. We may be sure that Paul interpreted them in the light of his Jewish background and his experience with Christ.

Christian thought and action is to be determined by the "true" rather than that which is false, unreal, and deceptive. "Honorable" describes that which is worthy of respect. Conduct and relationships are to be governed by what is "just" or upright and by that which is characterized by moral purity. The "lovely" is anything that is worthy of love.

The word translated "gracious" means literally "that which is spoken well of" ("of good report"—KJV). It is translated "admirable" in the NIV.

Paul specifically mentioned six virtues. These are followed by two general characteristics. Believers are to commit themselves to anything which is excellent and "worthy of praise." The word translated "excellence" has the usual meaning of "virtue."

According to the RSV, Paul urged his readers to "think about" these positive, constructive virtues. But the word does not mean just to reflect on them. Another translation has the more forceful "fill all your thoughts with these things" (NEB). Paul was concerned about the concrete expression in life and action of the characteristics mentioned. The emphasis in verse 9 is on doing. The pattern for action is what the community has learned and observed from Paul's own teachings and life.

Gratitude for a Gift (4:10-13)

For the first time in the letter Paul mentioned the gift of money sent to him by the Philippians through Epaphroditus. Why did Paul delay his expression of thanks and give so little attention to the gift itself? A logical explanation has been offered by some scholars. Either orally or by means of a previous letter, Paul had already conveyed his thanks to his friends. After all, it had apparently been some months since the gift had arrived, and Paul had had previous contacts with the church during that time.

"Blossomed afresh" (NEB) captures the meaning of the verb in verse 10 better than "revived." Paul immediately sensed that his statement of gratitude could be misunderstood. He let his readers know that he was aware that the length of time between their expressions of love was due to lack of "opportunity" rather than lack of willingness.

Paul also wanted to make clear his relationship to material things. He was grateful for the love expressed by the Philippians in their gift. But he wanted them to know that his own Christian faith and joy did not fluctuate with the material circumstances of his life. His contentment was the same in times of need as in times of plenty.

It has often been said that Paul's statement in verses 11-12 is very similar to Stoic thought. In verse 13, however, we see the difference between him and the Stoics. They cultivated an attitude of indifference toward the circumstances of life, and their strength was due to their own resources. Paul's strength, however, came as a result of his "in Christ" relationship. The secret of his contentment in difficult circumstances was Christ.

The context of verse 13 shows clearly that Paul was not talking about his accomplishments. There were certainly some things Paul could not do. There were certain factors which bore upon his life which he could not change. But whatever the problem, difficulty, or disappointment, Paul found in Christ the strength to face it. Specifically, he had the strength to bear up under economic hardship.

The Philippians' Partnership in the Gospel (4:14-20)

"Share" (v. 14) and "entered into partnership" (v. 15) are forms of the same word. The concept of partnership or fellowship is very important in Paul's thought.

The word for "trouble" (v. 14) is a special word in Paul's vocabulary. It does not refer to just any kind of trouble. It is the suffering or affliction which the Christian experiences as a result of his loyalty to Christ. One way the Philippians could have a part in Paul's trouble was by making a sacrificial gift to help alleviate any physical need. But more important than the money was the affirmation and love. Paul knew that he was not alone in his suffering.

Evidently the Philippians were unique among Paul's churches. From the outset they had expressed love to him through their gifts. "In the beginnings of the gospel" refers to the gospel's beginning in Philippi.

"Partnership with me in giving and receiving" expresses one of Paul's major ideas about the church. Believers bring what they have to the fellowship of the body and receive from it what they lack. The Philippians had received from Paul. Through him they had heard the gospel. They had given material gifts to Paul at least twice previously during his ministry in Thessalonica (Acts 17:1 ff.).

The money itself was not important to Paul, but the Christian spirit and generosity of the Philippians were. In this passage Paul used terms of business and finance. He was not concerned about "the gift" but about "the fruit" or interest which accrued from the gift. Interestingly enough, the profit from a gift accrues to the giver. He benefits the most from his investment.

The word for "credit" (v. 17) may also be rendered "account." By exercising generosity the Philippians would increase more in what really mattered: Christian love. There are always two aspects to this matter of the support of the ministry. The congregation gives what it has to take care of the needs of those who minister to it. But perhaps even more important is the growth of the congregation's Christian generosity through giving. Generosity is a Christian virtue; stinginess is an evil, whether it relates to ministerial support or any other aspect of the Christian life.

Paul wanted the Philippians to know that he did not expect anything else from them. Whatever they owed to him, they could consider the bill paid in full. "Received full payment" is a technical financial expression often found on receipts of the period.

Now Paul turned to the language of sacrifice to express the meaning of the Philippians' generosity. Their gift to him was really an "offering" to God. They could be sure that he was pleased with it and accepted it.

Paul was unable to reciprocate. But he believed that the God whom he served would "supply every need" of his friends. God's giving knows no limits, for it is "according to his riches." God's storehouse is inexhaustible. The nature of the riches is further qualified by the phrase "in glory." This is not a material, worldly, and therefore limited storehouse. There also may be the idea that real payment will be given in glory beyond this life. This is all modified by the phrase "in Christ Jesus." It is because of their relationship to God through Christ that believers can have confidence in receiving the riches of his grace.

Fittingly, Paul ended this passage with a doxology. God is the source of all good things. It was the love of God which was expressed in the Philippians' gift. The last word, therefore, is one of eternal praise to God.

The Conclusion (4:21-23)

The final word of greeting is typical. "Every saint in Christ Jesus" is everyone who trusts in Christ. Paul used the word where we often employ the term *Christian.* The reference to "Caesar's household" reinforces the conclusion that Paul was in prison in Rome. We cannot be dogmatic about this, however, because Caesar's servants were found throughout the empire.

We see here, however, that the gospel had penetrated even into the ranks of those who served the emperor. This may have been the result of Paul's own faithful witness during the time he was Caesar's prisoner.

COLOSSIANS

Introduction

Colossae was a textile center located in the upper Lycus Valley, in western Asia Minor (modern Turkey). Its neighboring cities were Laodicea and Hieropolis.

Paul had never visited those cities. He himself wrote that the Colossian and Laodicean believers did not know him personally (Col. 2:1). We may assume that the gospel had reached Colossae in relationship to missionary activity supervised by Paul during his long residence in Ephesus (Acts 19:1 ff.). Epaphras had served as Paul's helper in the evangelization of the first Colossian believers (Col. 1:7).

Place of Writing

Paul was in prison when he wrote his epistle to the Colossians (Col. 4:3). Traditionally it has been assumed that this imprisonment was in Rome (Acts 28:14 ff.). In modern times this tradition has been questioned, and scholars have advanced other hypotheses. Some have suggested Caesarea, while others have argued for Ephesus as the place where the imprisonment epistles were written. (See introduction to Philippians.) Although it is not vital to the interpretation of the letter, we shall assume that the traditional position is correct. This would place the date of writing in the early sixties.

The Occasion of the Letter

The churches in the Lycus Valley had been subjected to teachings considered by Paul to be subversive of the gospel and dangerous to the faith. The letter does not give enough information to enable us to give a precise account of the heresy. Certain aspects of it, however, will emerge for our study.

Apparently the heresy was a mixture of Christian, Jewish, and pagan ideas. Christ had a role in the false teaching, but he was considered to be only a partial manifestation of God. Other angelic principalities and powers also existed. In keeping with religious ideas of the times, the principalities and powers were probably thought of as astral deities, associated with the planets. The fullness of God was the sum of all these powers, including Christ. Essential knowledge of God also came from these other sources.

The Colossian heresy contained ascetic and cultic elements which had to be observed. Certain food and drink were forbidden (2:16). Certain holy days had to be observed (2:16). The body had to be brought under control by severe denial (2:23). Revelations through visions may have played an important part (2:18).

The Message of Colossians

In his letter Paul emphasized that Christ was sufficient for the total Christian life from beginning to end. Only he is worthy of worship and obedience, for the fullness of God is in him and in him alone (1:15-20). Believers needed no other source of understanding and knowledge (2:2).

The worship of the principalities and powers is both evil and foolish, for Christ is supreme in his authority over all of them (1:16). The unity and growth of the church depended on its faithful relationship to Christ, who is its head (2:19).

We know from Paul's letters that he was able to tolerate a great diversity of opinion and beliefs in the Christian body. But he resisted fiercely any teaching that denied to Christ his unique place as the only Savior and Lord of the church.

The church at Colossae had indeed held firm to its initial faith in Christ (2:15). Paul must have feared, however, that the Colossians could yet be seduced by false teachings. He wrote his letter, therefore, to encourage them to remain true to Christ and to assure them that they had in him all that they needed to live and grow in their faith.

The Genuine Gospel

1:1 to 2:5

The Salutation (1:1-2)

As was usual in letters of the first century, Paul began his letters with his own name as the writer of the epistle. He described himself as "an apostle of Christ Jesus." The word "apostle" means one who is sent. It could be used in a general sense as a delegate or messenger dispatched by an individual or a group. For example, Epaphroditus was the "messenger" (the word is apostle) of the Philippian church (Phil. 2:25).

But when he used "apostle" as a title for himself, Paul was thinking of a special group of people. They were the men who had been commissioned personally by the risen Lord and who represented him in a special way. Paul was the last of the apostles. His experience differed from those who had been with Jesus during his earthly ministry. But his apostleship was no less valid than theirs.

Paul was convinced that what happened to him outside Damascus was God's own doing. It was because of "the will of God" that he had been made an apostle of Christ Jesus.

Timothy was one of Paul's closest companions in much of his missionary work. A native of Lystra, he had joined Paul and Silas on the second missionary journey (Acts 16:1-3). Although he was Paul's junior in age and functioned as his helper, Paul spoke of him here as "our brother."

The epistle is addressed to the church in Colossae, a city in southwestern Asia Minor. This church had probably come into existence during Paul's ministry in Ephesus (Acts 19:10).

Paul described the Colossian church members as "saints." The word meaning "saints" or "holy ones" does not emphasize the moral achievements of believers. It underlines the fact that they are God's people. Anything or anyone who belongs to God is holy.

The Colossians were also "faithful brethren." All Christians belong to the family of God. Because of this, they are all brothers and sisters. In our translation the emphasis is placed on the loyalty or faithfulness of the family of God.

"Grace to you and peace" is the typical greeting in Paul's letters. Grace is God's undeserved favor and love by which we are saved and because of which we continue to be his people. Peace is the new state of existence made possible by grace. We are reconciled to God and to one another. Where hostility was the order of the day, peace now rules. Both grace and peace are continuing gifts "from God our Father."

Prayer of Thanksgiving (1:3-5a)

First-century letters began with the name of the writer, the name of the recipient, and a word of greeting. Often a prayer also followed. You can see that Paul followed this structure at the beginning of the letter. After the word of greeting, he included a prayer.

The first word is one of thanksgiving to God for the good things in the church. Paul knew that God was responsible for the accomplishments of the church. He was especially thankful for two aspects of the church's life. The first was their "faith." The second was their "love."

Faith and love were closely related in Paul's mind. You cannot really trust Jesus Christ without loving his people. They are two sides of the same coin. The Colossians were distinguished by love "for all the saints."

The quality of their life together as a church was determined by the "hope" which believers had. Here hope is not the subjective attitude but is the thing for which the believers hoped. In a word, it is their inheritance in glory. Paul said this inheritance was already "laid up" for the believers "in heaven." This emphasized the certainty of their future, guaranteed by the will of God.

The Fruit of the Gospel (1:5b-8)

Their hope is the one the Colossians had heard about when the gospel had been proclaimed to them. As we shall see, false ideas were being promoted among the Colossians. For this reason Paul emphasized the fact that the gospel which they had first heard was the true one. It contained all they needed for this life and the life to come.

The evidence of the authenticity and completeness of the gospel was its effect. It was "bearing fruit and growing" among the Colossians and in all other places where it had been accepted. Paul did not have numerical growth in mind. The proof of the gospel's adequacy is not in the numbers who accept it. Indeed, popularity can mean that the genuine gospel is not being preached.

Paul was talking about the effect of the gospel in the lives of the believers. False teachers were probably telling the Colossians that their original commitment was good, but it was not enough. They needed to accept new ideas in addition to the gospel if they were to expand and grow in their knowledge of God. To this Paul said an emphatic no in Colossians. The good news about Jesus Christ was all they needed to begin the Christian life and to live it through to the end.

Paul was not responsible personally for preaching the gospel to Colossae. That had been done by Epaphras, a native of the city. We gather, however, that Epaphras had worked under Paul's direction during his Ephesian ministry. As Paul put it, he had served Christ faithfully "on our behalf."

Epaphras had been the source of Paul's firsthand information about the church in Colossae. He had talked to Paul about their "love in the Spirit." For Paul the one universal manifestation of the Spirit's presence and power in the Christian's life was love.

Prayer of Intercession (1:9-12)

In his prayer Paul moved from thanksgiving to intercession. There was much in the church to bring joy. But the Christians in Colossae had not reached the maximum of their new life.

Paul's first request was for his readers to "be filled with the knowledge of his will." They had some understanding of God's will, but Paul longed for that understanding to be complete.

Too often we think of the will of God as a plan traced out for the individual life. We think of it in terms of career choices, marriage, changing jobs, and so forth. This concept has little support in the New Testament. The will of God in the broadest sense is his plan to redeem his people. In a narrower sense it has to do with the way we fit into that plan as individuals.

In order to know God's will we need the Spirit's gift of "wisdom and understanding." This is the God-given capacity to perceive what God is about and what he wants us to do. We cannot know God's will through our own efforts and capacity.

In verse 10 we see the individual outcome of knowing the will of God. It is that believers may "lead a life worthy of the Lord." The emphasis here is on the quality of life.

We know that God wants us to be honest, loving, loyal, generous, and kind, whatever may be the outward circumstances of our lives. Only in this way can we please him by "bearing fruit."

The second request is for "power." People need to know what God wants them to do. They also need the strength to live by the will of God. Paul believed that the possibilities of spiritual power were unlimited for the believer. God strengthens us "according to his glorious might."

The uses made of this power are very practical. It will guarantee "endurance and patience." "Endurance" translates a word which describes the believer's stance toward the difficult circumstances of his life. If he follows the will of the Lord, the Christian will encounter difficulty and hardship. But God gives him strength to face hardship with a victorious spirit.

"Patience" translates a word that describes the attitude of the believer toward difficult people. It is above all the way God relates to us. He does not give up on us. When we slip and fall, he is patient with us. The believer who has spiritual strength displays this patience toward other people.

"Joy" sounds the positive note. For us endurance and patience may have negative connotations. We may think in terms of bearing up or putting up with circumstances and people. But this is not the attitude of the believer supplied with the invincible power of God. The keynote of endurance and patience is joy, not gloomy resignation.

"Giving thanks" is another keynote of the Christian's life. Paul emphasized the importance of gratitude over and over again. Even when things are difficult, Christians are to be grateful. Their gratitude is a response to the love and goodness of God, who has made them what they are.

As Paul expressed it, we are to be grateful because God "qualified us (or made us fit) to share in the inheritance of the saints." The glorious future we have is due solely to God's work of grace in our lives.

Deliverance Through the Son (1:13-14)

What has God done to make us fit to share in glory? "He has delivered us from the dominion of darkness." In this phrase we perceive Paul's estimate of the human situation. Man in sin is a helpless victim, ruled over by dark and evil powers. He cannot free himself. What he needs is deliverance, and God has provided this.

Moreover, God has transported believers to a new sphere, the one in which his "beloved Son" reigns as King. For Paul there were only two possibilities of existence. The individual was either the slave of evil powers or a subject of Jesus Christ the heavenly King.

With the mention of "beloved Son," Paul focused his attention on the major theme of Colossians. The central teaching is about the person of Jesus Christ who is all-sufficient for the past, the present, and the future.

In Jesus Christ we have "redemption." The word translated "redemption" meant to set free upon the payment of a ransom and

was used of slaves, prisoners of war, and criminals. The emphasis in
the word as used by Paul is on liberation. In Christ we have been
freed from the power of sin (TEV).

Another way to speak of this is seen in the phrase "forgiveness of
sins." Helpless, hopeless, sinful we were. But God has saved us by
freely forgiving our sins. Paul used all the words and metaphors at
his command to drive this point home.

The All-Sufficient Son (1:15-20)

Who is this beloved Son? We can read between the lines of Colossians and perceive that there were some whose view of Christ was
not so lofty as Paul's. They promoted a doctrine in which Christ was
only one manifestation of God's power. Angelic powers existed which
believers also needed to worship and serve. Paul's description of Christ
is designed to rule out that kind of teaching.

Paul said that the Son was "the image of the invisible God." The
word translated "image" does not mean just a replica or a likeness.
The reality itself is present in the image. God himself, the invisible
one, had become visible and accessible to men through Jesus Christ.
Paul could not have made any loftier claim for Christ than to speak
of him as the image of God.

With relation to creation, Christ is the "first-born." This does not
mean, as some heretical groups have claimed, that Christ was the
first created being. Firstborn is a title of position and power. Christ
has preeminence over all the rest of creation just as the firstborn
has the position of authority in the family.

From the beginning to end, creation owes its existence to Christ.
All things were created "in him," "through him," and "for him . . .
whether thrones or dominions or principalities or authorities." The
average modern reader of the New Testament does not know that
these were words used in the ancient world for angelic or heavenly
powers. These were the kinds of powers that some false teachers
were urging the Colossians to worship. However, Christ as Creator
is superior to them.

Jesus Christ is not to be set alongside any other power. He and
he alone is the "head" of his "body" the "church." There are no
other rivals. He stands at the beginning; he is first; he is preeminent.
It was his victory over death that assured the victory of his followers.
Therefore, he is the "first-born from the dead." Again, "firstborn"
emphasizes preeminence, authority, and power. The emphasis is not

on first in time, although the resurrection of Jesus is the first of its kind and the opening victory over the power of death. But Jesus reigns also as Lord in the realm of the resurrected ones.

In all this Paul was trying to say in every way possible that Jesus Christ stands by himself, above and ahead of any other person or power. No other power can share his position. He and he alone is worthy of the worship and praise of mankind.

There are two remaining statements. The first has to do with Christ's nature as the revealer of God. "In him all the fullness of God was pleased to dwell." The false teachers apparently believed that Christ was only a partial revelation of God or that God was only partially present in Christ. In order to comprehend the fullness of God, people had to understand that he was represented by other powers. Paul emphatically denied this.

The second statement has to do with God's purpose in Christ. The universe was fragmented and broken. Paul understood this in cosmic terms. Not only were there hostile people, but there were also rebellious powers that were against God. God's purpose in Christ is to bring the universe fragmented by rebellion and sin back together, to restore the primeval harmony that had existed in the beginning.

The event through which this great universal peace is to be achieved is the death of Christ on the cross. We do not need another Savior or another saving event. In this one Savior and through his death alone God has determined to accomplish his total purpose of reconciliation.

God's Purpose Seen in the Church (1:21-23)

What is the evidence that God's purpose is reconciliation and that this purpose is achieved through the event of Christ's death? The answer lies right at hand. It is the experience of the church in Colossae. The Colossian Christians could well remember that they had been "estranged" from God. They had been at war against God.

This situation had been changed. They had been "reconciled" to God. What had brought them to God was the message that the incarnate Christ had died for them on the cross.

But the purpose of God in Christ had not been exhausted in their conversion. It looked toward the future when the Colossian believers would be presented to God as the people God intended them to be, without blame or reproach.

Verse 23 says you are responsible for your loyalty to Christ and his gospel. You can't believe what you want or do what you want and still be saved.

In the context of Colossians Paul was warning his readers not to be taken in by false doctrine. They needed to hold to the "hope of the gospel" which they had heard. They needed to resist any attempt to get them to shift their allegiance from Christ. This is the universal gospel, "preached to every creature under heaven." The one gospel is for all people.

The Ministry of Paul (1:24-29)

The good news that God had acted to achieve his purpose of reconciliation through Jesus Christ was the gospel for Paul. This was the message which he had been called to proclaim as a "minister" of the gospel.

This passage shows us how Paul viewed his ministry. Suffering had been an inescapable part of it. Paul spoke of "my sufferings for your sake." Paul believed that God had acted through Jesus Christ to save all people, Jews and Gentiles. Because of his commitment to this he had been hounded, stoned, beaten, and imprisoned. But the church in Colossae, a Gentile church, had come into being because Paul had been faithful to the genuine gospel of salvation by grace and not by law.

Paul wrote about completing what was "lacking in Christ's afflictions for the sake of his body." He believed that Christ had suffered and that through his sufferings the church had become a possibility. Christ's sufferings were unique and special. But if the purpose of God was to become a reality, others like Paul also had to be willing to suffer. Christ's servants have to share in his sufferings. Paul's attitude about this is positive: "I rejoice in my sufferings."

Paul believed that his role or "divine office"—that is, his apostolic ministry—was a gift to him from God. His task as an apostle was to make the word of God, the gospel, "fully known." Paul did not view his task as merely getting people converted or started on the road to salvation. They also needed to understand how their lives were to be lived by the gospel until they reached the final goal.

Paul said that the word of God had been a "mystery hidden" from previous generations. It was only through the revelation in Jesus Christ that God showed people what his eternal purpose was. The prophets had grasped it dimly and from afar. But only the "saints" or Christians could really grasp what Paul had been talking about.

What is this "mystery" or divine secret? It is the revelation that God's reconciling purpose in Christ included the Gentiles. Christ was also in them. Paul could also have said the Spirit of Christ or the Holy Spirit. The presence of Christ through his Spirit in Gentile believers was the proof that they had been included in God's plan. His presence in them was also their "hope of glory." They knew that they were going to share in the inheritance of the saints because Christ abided in them.

What is the Christian message about? It is about Christ. He is the beginning, center, and end of it. The "warning" mentioned by Paul was the admonition not to turn away from Christ to worship some other power. It is only as life is lived in him, subject to his will and direction, that Christians will become "mature." The goal of the Christian life is maturity. We start out as babes; but if we continue to live in relationship to Christ, he will bring us to full Christian growth or maturity.

Paul did not take any credit at all for what he had done. It had all been due to the "energy and power of Christ at work" in him (NEB).

Paul's Desire for the Church (2:1-5)

From 2:1 we learn for the first time that Paul was not personally acquainted with the Christians in Colossae or in Laodicea, a neighboring city to Colossae. Yet he spoke of his strenuous efforts on their behalf. And he spoke of this in the present tense. Was this a struggle in prayer? It must have been some kind of inward, spiritual struggle which Paul continued to experience for those Gentile churches even while he was in prison.

Paul expressed his ambition for the church in Colossae. In the first place, he hoped that there would be a unity in the church that comes from love. This is the love of God mediated through Jesus Christ, present in the church through the ministry of his Spirit. The second goal is an outgrowth of the first. Paul wanted them to have the full assurance that in Christ they possessed all that God had to give them.

As Paul put it, God had "hid all the treasures of wisdom and knowledge" in Christ. This is said in opposition to the beguiling, false teaching. Some people evidently taught that there were other sources of wisdom and knowledge. Paul warned his readers against being deluded by the attractive new teachings which had surfaced in their midst.

From verse 5 we learn that the church had indeed resisted the false teachings that would reduce the status and role of Christ in their faith. "Good order" and "firmness" were used in military terminology to describe the army that maintained its discipline and its ranks against the attack of the enemy. So the church in Colossae was apparently in good shape.

The Colossian Heresy

2:6 to 3:4

Warning Against Danger (2:6-8)

By way of anticipation we have already referred to a false teaching which had been presented to the church at Colossae, which evidently had been rejected by the members. In chapter 2 some of the false teachings which troubled Paul may be identified.

First, there is the positive injunction. The Colossians had "received Christ" at the beginning of their Christian lives. Contrary to all the notions with which they had been bombarded, he was all they needed to develop and grow as Christians.

The KJV "walk" is a literal translation of the verb which means "live" (2:6). This verb encompasses every aspect of living or conduct—thoughts, actions, relationships, and speech. The life of the believer is to be lived totally "in Christ"—that is, in relationship to him. He furnishes the motivation, the pattern, and the energy needed for Christian living.

The translations have difficulty bringing out the force of the various tenses of the verbs in verses 6 and 7. "Live," "built up," and "established" are in the present tense. They emphasize ongoing aspects of the believer's life. We have not reached the maximum of Christian growth, stability, or maturity in our faith.

"Rooted" is in the perfect tense. It refers to something which happened in the past but which continues to exercise an influence in the present. At their conversion the Colossians were rooted in Christ. This condition still existed. They did not need another source of life and nourishment. They needed to grow as they drew upon the resources of Christ.

Verse 8 contains the warning against being misled by the false teaching. The central problem of the verse centers around the word translated "elemental spirits." The word can also refer to basic elements, rudiments, principles, the *ABC*'s of anything.

Scholars, however, generally accept the idea reflected in the RSV translation. The word was used in the ancient world to refer to astral deities, heavenly powers that controlled human life and destiny. This is probably a reference to the central teaching of the heresy in Colossae. According to the heretics, there were elemental spirits besides Christ that needed to be worshiped and, perhaps, placated.

The teachers of this heresy probably made bold claims for it. They called it a "philosophy." They said that it came from God. They held that their teaching was the source of genuine knowledge and wisdom. Paul said it was empty, deceitful, and from human rather than heavenly sources. For Paul anything "not according to Christ" was to be rejected.

Fullness in Christ (2:9-15)

There is no need for believers to seek anything outside Christ because they have everything in him. This is the basic proposition in Colossians, and it is given clear expression in verses 9-10. The "fulness of deity" dwells in Christ. God's power and wisdom are not distributed among various angelic beings, of whom Christ is only one. "Bodily" may refer to the incarnation. God in his fullness was revealed to humanity in the incarnate Christ.

Since God comes to believers fully in Jesus Christ, they receive "fulness of life" when they accept him. This does not mean at all that they become in that moment what they are meant to be. It does mean that nothing else is needed to augment what they have in Christ.

To describe the absolute adequacy of what Christ has brought to the Colossian Christians, Paul used the figures of circumcision and baptism. Presumably the Colossians were Gentiles. They had not been circumcised physically. But Paul described their experience of conversion as a circumcision. In this experience they had put off the "body of flesh." "Flesh" has various meanings in Scripture. Here, as in many other places, it stands for the old life of rebellion against God. Paul spoke of flesh as a power that rules the life in opposition to the power of God's Spirit. When they became Christians, the Colossians were freed from that power. This is the "circumcision of Christ," the one that he performs on the believer.

Next Paul wrote about baptism. The Colossians, of course, had been baptized. Christian baptism is equated by Paul with dying and being buried. Christ died and was buried in a tomb. We die and are buried with him in a watery grave. This means that there is a radical dividing line between what the Christian now is and what he used to be. He not only died, but he is raised with Christ.

Note that the decisive phrase in verse 12 is "through faith." Paul did not believe that the physical act of being put under the water changed a person any more than physical circumcision. What is important is our trust in God. What is even more important is what God does for the believer. God makes him "alive."

A "bond" was a note of indebtedness written in the debtor's own hand and signed personally by him. Paul seemed to be saying that unsaved humanity has an "IOU" outstanding against it. What is this bond? It is something which contains "legal demands." Interpreters generally conclude that Paul had the Jewish law in mind. If this is true, we are not saved by fulfilling the law. We are saved because our debt as described by the law has been "canceled." How did God set it aside? He did so by nailing it to the cross. That is a bold way of saying that our liberation comes only through the death of Jesus Christ.

Not only did the cross render our indebtedness null and void. It also represented the victory of Christ over "the principalities and powers." Once again we apparently have a reference to those angelic powers which some people said Christians should also worship. According to the RSV translation, Christ "disarmed the principalities and powers." Another possible understanding of the difficult phrase is found in the TEV: "Christ freed himself from the power of the spiritual rulers and authorities." (See also the NEB.) The idea lying behind this is that the powers attempted to destroy Christ by killing him, but his death was really his victory over them and not theirs over him.

Because of what Christ did, the powers do not have any authority over Christians. In describing the work of Christ, the apostle made use of a well-known event—the triumphal return of the military conqueror from battle. Some other translations make the picture of verse

15 clearer than the RSV—for example, "he made a public spectacle of them by leading them as captives in his victory procession" (TEV).

The Errors of False Teachings (2:16-23)

We have noted the central error of the false teaching in Colossae. It was the failure to recognize the sufficiency of Jesus Christ to meet all the needs of believers. Now some other elements of the teaching come to light.

For one thing the heresy gave great importance to dietary laws. Certain foods and drink were forbidden. We believe also that there are certain things which the Christian should not take into his body. The reason for this is that they are injurious to health, and the decision is based upon scientific data. But for the Christian there is no food that is clean or unclean in itself, in the sense that it is contaminated spiritually. As Jesus said, we are defiled not by what goes into the body but by what comes out of our hearts (Mark 7:18-20).

The heresy also placed great emphasis on holy days. We are not told the basis for the dietary laws or the religious calendar. Most people think that much of it was based upon Jewish concepts and practices. Paul did not believe in holy days. He believed that all of life is holy. For Christians every day is holy in the sense that it is offered up to the Lord.

Paul held that the reality of the Christian life was not determined by holding to dietary laws or observing holy days. These are "a shadow of what is to come." There seems to be no question here but that he was thinking of the Old Testament. Paul believed that those laws about foods and holy days pointed forward to the reality of Christ. The person who has Christ does not need to worry about keeping those laws.

Verse 18 is one of the most difficult in the New Testament to translate and interpret. The RSV translation is as good as any. Two aspects of the heresy seem to surface here—an emphasis on the worship of angels and on revelations from God through visions. "Self-abasement" is probably a derogatory reference to people who taught that true humility would cause us to worship angelic powers superior to us.

"Disqualify" comes from the athletic games. A referee could disqualify a contestant who broke the rules.

In verse 19 Paul came back to the basic problem. The false teachers are "not holding fast to the Head." The only criterion for being Christian is one's relationship to Jesus Christ as Savior and Lord. By pushing their doctrine of angel worship, the enemies of the gospel were really disqualifying themselves. Christ and Christ alone is the source of nourishment for the body, his church. He and he alone is the reason for its unity. He holds it together. When believers hold "fast to the Head," they receive what they need as the body of Christ to grow into that maturity which is God's goal for his church.

Connected with the worship of the "elemental spirits" were certain taboos. There were things, not specified by Paul, that the worshipers were forbidden to "handle," "taste," or "touch." Since believers had died "with Christ" to the powers, they had nothing to fear from taboos associated with them. The powers had no authority over those who lived under Christ's power in the new life.

Paul criticized the dietary laws and other taboos from two perspectives. First, they relate to material things that "perish as they are used." Thus they have no eternal significance. Second, such prohibitions come from "human precepts and doctrines" rather than from God.

Verse 23 is difficult to translate, as you can see by comparing various versions. The idea, however, is clear. Asceticism always has a certain appeal. To deny oneself certain foods and drinks can serve to indicate one's rigorous "devotion." It can also be used to prove that a person has his "body" under control. Paul did not believe, however, that the "flesh" could be checked by imposing legalistic taboos. The flesh describes for Paul that which is at enmity against God. It can be dealt with only from within, through the power of God's Spirit.

The New Life in Christ (3:1-4)

People are not changed by imposing legalistic restrictions on what they eat or drink. They are changed by the power of God. This change, which takes place at conversion, is so radical that Paul can speak of it as death and resurrection with Christ.

The translation of 3:1 in the RSV can leave the wrong impression. Substitute "since" for "if." It was because the Colossian Christians had been raised to new life that they were able to pursue higher goals. This is the exact opposite of the teaching criticized by Paul. They were being told: "Do this and you will live." Paul taught: "Because you already have life, you are to do what God wants you to do."

"Things that are above" are not matters of geography, of course. Paul does not specify what they are here, but they would certainly have to do with a life of trust and love. "Things that are on the earth" would be lower, passing, worldly values and goals. In the verses which follow, Paul wrote about the characteristics of the higher and lower life.

Christians cannot now know fully the genuine nature and richness of their lives. That "is hid" from them because their life is really in Christ. At his appearing they will enter into "glory," the eternal existence of the redeemed. Then they will become fully aware of the riches of the life God had given to them. He believed that the culmination of God's redemptive purpose for his people would come at that moment when their Lord appeared.

The Higher *vs.* the Lower Life

3:5 to 4:6

The Old Nature and the New (3:5-11)

Christians have always had to deal with the problem of immorality and evil within the ranks of the church itself. We can be sure that Christians were guilty of the kinds of sins that Paul wrote about. Otherwise, there would have been no point in what he wrote.

God had done his part. He had raised the believers to new life. In the light of this they had a moral responsibility to conduct themselves in keeping with their new existence. That responsibility is to "put to death" all that is "earthly."

Paul gave two lists of earthly things, each list consisting of five evils. The first list (v. 5) contains the kinds of evils which Christians generally think of as earthly, fleshly, or carnal. The emphasis is on sexual sins, both the overt expression in "fornication" and the kinds of inner impulses which lead to sexual immorality, such as "passion" and "evil desire." Also "covetousness" or greed is mentioned. It is equated with "idolatry." The inordinate desire for things is in essence the worship of false gods.

The second list of sins (v. 8) emphasizes wrong attitudes and wrong relations with other people. For Paul "anger, wrath, malice, slander, and foul talk" (abusive language) were just as much sins of the flesh as was fornication. We have not always understood this. In our churches drunkenness or sexual immorality often disqualifies one from being a Sunday School teacher. Gossip, on the other hand, may not. But gossip is just as earthly as is drunkenness.

These sins are the cause of the coming "wrath of God." Paul believed that such evils should be taken seriously by God's people because God takes them seriously. To a great extent we have lost the sense of the tragedy of sin today.

Before their conversion the Christians in Colossae had "walked" in the sins mentioned by Paul. This means that their conduct had been determined by them. But at that time as unredeemed sinners they "lived in them." This means that their very existence was found in that sphere of evil.

Now, however, a change had taken place. They lived in the sphere ruled over by Christ. Their conduct, therefore, should be consistent with their new lives. To be Christians and to behave according to the old patterns was a contradiction. Life and conduct needed to be in harmony.

We fail to understand Paul's morality unless we perceive that it was a social morality. The new life of the believer meant that he had entered a relationship with the people of God. The pattern of this relationship was radically new and different. The "practices" of the "old nature" were characterized by deceit, dishonesty, and lying. Believers had "put off the old nature." They had "put on the new nature." The metaphor is that of changing clothing. They had taken off the old; they had put on the new.

This meant that their relationship with others had a totally different character. Openness, candor, and honesty are its hallmarks. The relationship of believers is one of mutual trust and sincerity.

This new nature is not something that has power in itself. It is not something that can function separately and apart from God, who is its source. It is "being renewed." The tense is present and lays stress on the constant daily renewal of the Christian by God.

The "knowledge" mentioned by the apostle is knowledge of God. It is the personal knowledge of God who reveals his will and way to his child. The pattern of the renewal is the "image of the creator." Man was created in the image of God. He was exactly what God wanted him to be. But through sin he fell short of this glory. The purpose of God in the new creation is to achieve that which was frustrated by sin.

One major aspect of man's fall is the alienation, discord, and prejudice which divide men from one another. In pagan, sinful, rebellious society people are divided by race into "Greek and Jew." They are divided religiously into "circumcised and uncircumcised." They are divided socially and economically into "barbarian, Scythian, slave," and "free."

In the Mediterranean world a barbarian was a person who did not speak Greek, the dominant language of commerce and culture. Scythians were a nomadic, savage Indo-European group from South Russia that penetrated as far as Egypt in the seventh century BC. Their name had become synonymous with the extremes of barbarism and cruelty.

When God creates the new man, his own people, in Christ, all these divisions disappear. For the Christian, race, social status, and money lose all meaning. "Christ is all, and in all."

The Character of the New Nature (3:12-17)

Believers are God's "chosen" people. They belong to God as his redeemed community as a result of his saving initiative. As such, they are to be clothed with a new kind of life. Paul earlier talked about the old that must be put off. Now he talked about the new which is to be "put on." He listed five virtues which characterize the people of God.

We notice that the emphasis is on attitudes and actions which determine the believer's relationship to the community of the redeemed. Furthermore, this relationship is one of love. All the elements in the list speak about different ways of expressing the love of God that has become the central fact of the believer's life. The unbeliever makes himself the center of his life. His thought and efforts are directed toward himself. The Christian makes others the center of his life and subordinates his own desires and ambitions to the welfare of his brother. "Compassion, kindness, lowliness, meekness, and patience" reflect this radical change.

Paul was aware of the imperfections of the Christian community and, therefore, of the need for the spirit of Christ. We do not need the grace of God to love the lovely. Any pagan can do that. Grace is for those people and times when it is difficult to live the life of love.

Because Christians sometimes are difficult to live with, we need the grace of forbearance. People are prone to offend, so we need the grace of forgiveness. Notice the measure of forgiveness. We are to forgive each other "as the Lord has forgiven [us]." The determining factor in the Christian's relationship to others is the way the Lord has related to him.

"Above all these put on love." Everything that Paul has mentioned to this point is an aspect or expansion of love. Love is more important than anything else in the Christian life. It is not a sentiment or emotion. It is a way of acting. The definition of love is not left up in the air for the Christian. It is above all the love of God expressed in his redemption through Jesus Christ. It goes out to people who do not deserve it and acts in total disregard for its own welfare. This love must be put on "above all," for it is the identifying mark of the genuine believer.

The meaning of Paul's remark about love is unclear (v. 14). It probably means that love binds all the other virtues together so that they form a harmonious whole. There is another possibility. It binds all Christians together so that the church is what God wants it to be—that is, perfect or mature. In this case you would substitute "everybody" for "everything" in the RSV translation.

Not strife but peace is to be the characteristic of believers in their life together. This is the "peace of Christ," the peace which he gives by reconciling them to God and to one another. The heart is the inmost center of the individual—the seat of his will, intellect, and emotions. It is the center from which all human activity proceeds. That center is to be governed by Christ's peace.

One of the problems with us Christians is that we try to live lives of love and peace when there are hostilities, aggressions, and insecurities inside us that have not been dealt with. If Christ rules over this center, the periphery will take care of itself.

God's calling has made us "one body." Strife in that body is a contradiction of God's call and purpose. When peace rules in our hearts, the body is in fact what God called it to be.

Gratitude is another of the genuine marks of the Christian community. When Paul said, "Be thankful," he was not referring just to inward gratitude. He intended that the church express its gratitude in the services of worship and praise.

It is clear from verse 16 that Paul had the life of the church in mind. It is characterized by the indwelling "word of Christ." This is the genuine gospel which false teachers had attacked. It is the "word of Christ" alone that is to be central in the church's life.

When the word of Christ dwells in the church, three activities result. There is teaching. Instruction in the word of the Lord was evidently central from the beginning of Christian history. Then there is admonishing. Christians have a responsibility for the moral and spiritual lives of one another. They fulfill that responsibility in part by admonishing their brothers and sisters to help them with their weaknesses and failures. But this admonishing is really the application of Christ's own word to the lives of his people.

Third, singing as an expression of gratitude and worship is characteristic of the church's response to the word of her Lord. That word is above all the message of God's love and redemption in Jesus Christ.

We do not know the exact distinction among "psalms and hymns and spiritual songs." They refer, no doubt, to the whole range of early Christian music from the psalms of the Old Testament to songs of praise inspired by the Spirit (spiritual songs).

All Christian speech and all Christian action is to be in the name of "the Lord Jesus." The name stands for the person in biblical thought. The statement means, therefore, that all we do is to be done in terms of our relationship with Jesus.

Family Relationships (3:18 to 4:1)

Now Paul turned to some concrete advice about Christian living in the world of his day. Paul gave us the greatest expressions of the equal worth of all people found in the New Testament. We find these statements in Colossians 3:11 and Galatians 3:28. In Galatians Paul told us that there is "neither male nor female" in the body of Christ.

As far as Paul was concerned, therefore, all of the divisions which put people into inferior and superior groups were wrong and unworthy of the church. That is the Christian principle for the life of the church.

But what about life in society? How are Christians to behave there? Does the Christian principle mean that all restraints are to be thrown off and that there is no order at all? Apparently some problems were caused in those early days because people interpreted Christian liberty in that way.

Wives and husbands (3:18-19).—Paul believed that there was an order for the family. His conviction was not based upon notions of male superiority. It seems that he believed the order was God-given. In this order the husband functions as the head of the family. Paul taught that women were to be subject to their husbands. In this order the husband is to love his wife and not "be harsh" with her.

We must remember that the husband in many cases had the power of life and death over members of his family. Women and children were often subject to uncontrolled abuse. Paul spoke against that evil. If we see his teaching in this light, we can appreciate its real advance over contemporary patterns in his society.

Children and parents (3:20-21).—In the family children and parents have reciprocal responsibilities. Children are responsible for obeying their fathers. Fathers are not to misuse and abuse their parental authority. Authority is not to be expressed in an arbitrary and undisciplined way that will cause children to become frustrated and discouraged.

Slaves and masters (3:22 to 4:1).—We know from his explicit statements that Paul did believe that slavery belonged in God's order. In the church there is neither "slave nor free." But what was the Christian apostle to say to Christian slaves and Christian masters in the first-century Roman world?

To begin with, the Christian church was a tiny minority in a despotic society. Paul did not conceive the possibility that the pagan, evil society of his day might adopt Christian principles. Nor did he conceive the tiny Christian communities forcing that society to change its patterns by revolution.

Later, when Christianity was strong enough, God's word to believers through men like Livingstone and Wilberforce was: Abolish slavery. One of the tragedies of our own nation was that many of our political and religious leaders attempted to justify slavery. Some even taught that it was God's will.

Paul did not justify it. He did not think that the divisions were Christian. They were part of a pagan, passing order that was under the judgment of God. But he believed that the Christian gospel had to be lived out in the practical circumstances of everyday life. How are Christians to live, therefore, in an unjust world?

He told slaves to obey their "earthly masters." The key word is "earthly." Jesus was their real, eternal Lord. The relationship of slaves to their owners was temporary and passing. Obedience to masters was not a new idea. It was the general rule of society, enforced by harsh laws. What was new in Paul's approach was his view that Christian slaves could elevate their bondage by offering that up to the service of their Lord.

Because they were Christians, these slaves were to be different from others in three particulars. Their service was not grudging, outward conformity. Earthly masters cannot see beneath the surface. But the Christian's Lord sees the "heart," the center of will and intellect. "Singleness of heart" may be translated in various ways to bring out the meaning—for example, "single-mindedness" (NEB) and "sincerity of heart" (NIV). The Christian, as a Christian, is never hypocritical. There is always harmony between thought and action.

Second, Christian slaves were to regard their work as service to the Lord rather than to their earthly masters. Third, they were to live in the confidence that their real reward would come from the heavenly Master whom they served and not from men.

We are thankful that slavery has been abolished, largely through the influence of great Christian men and women. This passage still has an application, however, in that it sets forth some guiding principles for working people. The Christian worker can ennoble the working place through honest, sincere work which he offers up as a testimony to his Lord.

Paul also had a word for Christian "masters." It is shorter, probably because there were few Christian masters and many Christian slaves. There was much cruelty and abuse of slaves in the Roman empire. Christian masters were to be different. Justice and equality were to be the guiding principles of their conduct.

Masters were to be aware that they were also slaves—slaves to a heavenly master. In this respect both Christian slave and master stood on the same ground. They both had the same relationship to the eternal Lord. The differences between them were earthly and passing, and both were to be conscious of that.

Prayer and Behavior (4:2-6)

Prayer is a basic expression of the Christian faith. If we believe that God is personal, a heavenly Father who cares for us, we are going to pray. From this passage we learn something about the character and content of Christian prayer.

Three characteristics of prayer emerge from Paul's comments. They are steadfastness, alertness, and thanksgiving. Steadfast is the opposite of occasional. Some people pray only in times of personal crisis. But prayer is a constant part of the good Christian's life.

"Watchful" reminds us of Jesus' command to the disciples: "Watch and pray" (Mark 14:38). Prayer is one way to maintain vigilance.

And, of course, all Christian prayer is uttered in the spirit of thankfulness for what God has done, is doing, and is going to do for us through his Son.

The content of Paul's request for prayer is interesting. Paul was in prison, but he did not ask for anything for himself. His basic concern was for the gospel. He wanted the Colossians to make two things the burden of their prayer for him. He desired an "open . . . door"—that is, an opportunity to proclaim the gospel. Paul could call it the "mystery of Christ" since many people did not yet know the truth of God's redemption through Christ. He also wanted his fellow Christians to pray that he might take advantage of that opportunity by making the message "clear."

Next Paul wrote about the conduct of the community in terms of its relationship to "outsiders." These were, of course, the non-Christians. Believers are not to draw apart from the world in a little exclusive clique. They have a responsibility to represent the gospel to those who have not accepted it. Their conduct is to be characterized by wisdom. In the Bible wisdom is the God-given insight into God's will and purpose.

Believers are to make the "most of the time" in their relationship to pagans. The word "time" here really means the opportunities which are presented in time (see NEB). In their contact with unbelievers, God's people would have opportune moments to influence them for the gospel.

How is a person to speak to outsiders about the gospel? How is he to answer the questions raised by unbelievers? Paul did not give specific answers. He did admonish the Colossians to use speech that was "gracious, seasoned with salt." This means that believers are not to be dull and uninteresting in their presentation of the gospel.

Some people always have the same phrases and clichés to use on everybody they encounter. Both the example of Jesus and the advice of Paul indicate that this is wrong. People differ; situations differ. Christians who are sensitive will try to choose their words to fit the person and the circumstances.

Final Greetings
4:7-18

Paul's letters usually end much like the epistle to the Colossians. Here we find personal messages (4:7-9), greetings (vv. 10-15), and final instructions (vv. 16-17). The letter closes with a final greeting, written by Paul's own hand, and a brief benediction (v. 18).

The Bearers of the Letter (4:7-9)

We could wish that Paul had given us more detailed information about his own circumstances. Basically Paul was not concerned about his own problems. His central interest was the gospel.

There is another reason, however, for the lack of autobiographical detail. Paul sent his letters to the churches by personal messengers. They knew intimately what was happening to the apostle. He expected them to give a verbal report to the church about these matters. Writing materials were scarce and expensive in the ancient world. Writing itself was a laborious process. There would be a tendency on Paul's part, therefore, not to use writing materials to convey information which could be transmitted better orally.

The two messengers in this case were Tychicus and Onesimus. Tychicus, a native of the Roman province of Asia, was a member of the delegation who accompanied Paul on his last trip to Jerusalem (Acts 20:4). He is also mentioned in Ephesians 6:21; 2 Timothy 4:12; and Titus 3:12. Tychicus is described in three phrases. Because he was a member of the Christian family, he was a "brother." Because he had performed a specific work in the Christian cause, he was a "minister." His devotion and high sense of responsibility were underlined by the adjective "faithful." Because he lived with Paul under the lordship of Christ, he was a "fellow servant" (or, literally, slave).

Were it not for the little epistle called Philemon, we would not know who Onesimus really was. From that source, however, we learn that Onesimus was a runaway slave, a convert to the faith, and a close personal friend to the apostle. Paul was sending him back to his master in Colossae. Philemon was probably written and sent to Colossae along with this epistle.

In terms of earthly status Onesimus was a slave. There is no hint of that in Paul's comment in Colossians. To the apostle he was a "faithful and beloved brother." "One of yourselves" tells us that he was a native of Colossae.

Tychicus and Onesimus were to tell the Colossians about Paul. But the object was not to excite pity and concern for him—indeed, the opposite! Their purpose was pastoral, to "encourage" their "hearts" (v. 8). They were to make their report in such a way as to encourage and reassure the Colossians.

Messages of Greeting (4:10-15)

Some Christians in contact with Paul sent their greetings to the church in Colossae. The first mentioned is Aristarchus. He went with Paul on his final trip to Jerusalem (Acts 19:29; 20:4). He also accompanied the apostle when he was taken to Rome (Acts 27:2).

Paul called him a "fellow prisoner." This, however, is probably to be understood figuratively. The word for *prisoner* really means prisoner of war. It is different from the term used by Paul when referring to his actual imprisonment. The apostle meant that he and Aristarchus were prisoners of the Lord.

The second man, Mark, was a native of Jerusalem (Acts 12:12,25). He accompanied Paul and his cousin Barnabas on their first missionary trip. Because he deserted the traveling missionaries at Perga (Acts 13:13), Paul refused to take him on the next trip (Acts 15:37,39). Paul may have been somewhat hasty and harsh in his judgment of a younger John Mark. It is good to know that they became close friends and fellow workers in later years.

The third man bore the name Jesus (Joshua in Hebrew), a popular name among Jews in the first century. This Jesus was known in the Gentile world by his Roman name, Justus.

Aristarchus, Mark, and Justus were the only Jewish Christians ("men of the circumcision") in the vicinity who had remained faithful to Paul. Verse 11 has a note of bitterness and implies that others "of the circumcision" were hostile to Paul. Perhaps this was because they disagreed with his gospel of grace and the way he opened the doors of the church to Gentiles.

Epaphras, a native of Colossae, had been the pioneer missionary to the city (see 1:7). As the one who saw the church come into being, he was also interested in its maturity and assurance in the faith. Although he was not with them, he prayed for them to be "mature and fully assured in all the will of God." From this passage we learn that Epaphras had also labored in "Laodicea and Hierapolis." They were neighboring cities to Colossae.

The passage also tells us about all we really know of Luke. Since Paul did not include him among the "men of the circumcision," he must have been a Gentile. He was also a physician. According to early tradition, he was the author of the gospel that bears his name.

Demas is mentioned here as Paul's friend. In 2 Timothy 4:10, however, we read this sad, poignant commentary: "For Demas, in love with this present world, has deserted me."

Finally Paul sent his own greetings to the Christians in Laodicea and to a believing lady named Nympha. In those early days groups of Christians often assembled in the homes of certain Christians for worship. Nympha had such a group, commonly called a "house church," meeting in her home.

Final Instructions (4:16-18)

Paul wrote letters. But they were not personal, confidential epistles. They were intended for public reading in the churches. This was the first step down the road which led to these letters being accepted as Holy Scripture, inspired parts of the Christian Bible. Evidently Paul wrote a letter to the church at Laodicea at or about the same time that he wrote Colossians. Possibly the two letters were sent at the same time. He wanted both letters read publicly in both churches. We do not have an epistle to Laodicea in our New Testament. Many guesses have appeared about the identity of this letter. Some have suggested that it was our Ephesians, which is very similar to Colossians. Others think it may have been Philemon. Probably it has been lost, and we do not have it at all.

Paul wanted the church in Colossae to urge Archippus to "fulfil [a] ministry." Archippus is mentioned also in Philemon 2.

Paul wrote the final greeting in his own hand. Evidently he made this a practice to prevent the possibility of the kind of forgery that may have occurred at Thessalonica (2 Thess. 2:2; 3:17).

The apostle called upon the church to remember his "fetters." Probably what he had in mind was not his own personal suffering. He was in fetters as a prisoner of Christ. He was a prisoner because of his faithfulness to the gospel of grace. They were to remember his fetters in this context, with an awareness of their meaning and a commitment to it.

The last word is "grace." It also stands at the beginning of the letter. For Paul the great blessing of the church was grace. Its greatest continuing need was also for the constant outpouring of God's grace. It was redeemed, sustained, and given hope through grace—God's undeserved love in Jesus Christ.

1 THESSALONIANS

Introduction

Thessalonica, the chief city of Macedonia, was the seat of administration for the Roman province. Located on the gulf of Saloniki, it was also the leading seaport of Macedonia. It sat astride the Via Egnatia, one of the most important highways of the empire.

The Occasion of the Letter

On his so-called second missionary journey the apostle Paul, with his companions, Silvanus (Silas) and Timothy, made his way to Thessalonica (Acts 17:1 ff.). At that time the church came into being. Forced by persecution to leave the city, Paul journeyed to Athens (Acts 17:10 ff.).

All the while he was concerned about the ability of the new converts to stand up under the persecution to which they were being subjected. Unable to visit Thessalonica again himself, he dispatched Timothy to pay a visit to the church (3:2). His mission was to strengthen the believers and bring a report back to Paul about the condition of the congregation.

In the meantime, Paul traveled to Corinth. While he was there, Timothy returned to report that the church was standing up remarkably well under her affliction and gave witness to the reality of her relationship to the Lord in her faith, love, and hope.

Overjoyed with the news, Paul wrote and dispatched this first letter to Thessalonica. Through it he hoped to strengthen the church further to be faithful under the pressure to which it was still subjected and to reinforce the instruction for Christian living he had given during his ministry in the city.

Evidently Timothy reported that some of the believers were anxious about the fate of their brothers and sisters who had died. Paul sought to reassure them by teaching that those who died before the coming of the Lord would not be left out of that great event (4:13 to 5:4).

The Date of the Epistle

Through extant archaeological evidence we can date Paul's ministry in Corinth with precision and confidence. He spent eighteen months there between AD 49 and 52. First Thessalonians apparently was written during the first part of his Corinthian ministry. Therefore, the date was around AD 50.

The Reception of the Gospel in Thessalonica

1:1-10

The Salutation (1:1)

Paul began the letter with the name of the writer, the name of the recipient, a greeting, and a prayer of gratitude and intercession. This was the way letters generally began in the Hellenistic world of the first century. Paul was simply following the customary pattern.

There is one major difference, however, between Paul and his contemporaries. He normally added comments to the elements in the introduction of his letters which conveyed important ideas. Paul did less of this in the Thessalonian correspondence than in his other letters. The result is a very brief salutation.

For example, the names of the three men involved in writing the letter are given without the usual descriptive comments. In Acts Silvanus is called Silas. He was the companion of Paul on the so-called second missionary journey (Acts 15:40). Thus he was with Paul on the initial visit to Thessalonica (Acts 17:1 ff.).

Timothy joined Paul and Silas on the missionary journey which took the trio to Thessalonica (Acts 16:1-3). Later Paul dispatched Timothy to Thessalonica to see how the young congregation was faring. After Timothy's return and in response to his report, 1 Thessalonians was penned.

"Church" in the New Testament refers to the people and not the building. Also, we should not understand the word in the modern institutional sense. It is not the church belonging to the Thessalonians. It is the congregation of God's people composed of believing Thessalonians.

The church is described as being "in God the Father and the Lord Jesus Christ." The idea that Christians are "in God" or "in Christ" is typical of the apostle. Perhaps the meaning of the phrase in this context is that they belonged to God and to the Lord Jesus Christ (NEB). This is what made them a church.

The normal greeting in a Hellenistic letter was a word which we may translate "rejoice." Paul substituted for it two great Christian words. "Grace" is the love of God which flows toward us no matter who we are or what we have done. It is the reason for our salvation and our relationship to God. "Peace" describes this new relationship which exists between believer and God and among believers themselves. It is the total well-being which flows from the new life of grace.

Prayer of Gratitude (1:2-3)

Paul generally began his letters with a prayer of thanksgiving to God for the good things in the lives of his readers. An exception is the epistle to the Galatians, written in the heat of passion and disappointment.

Paul's prayers were inclusive; they were for "all" the Thessalonians. They were constant and continual. They were prayers of gratitude. The good things in the lives of the believers came from God. Therefore Paul thanked God for them instead of bragging on the believers themselves.

What caused Paul to be so grateful to God? It was the "faith," "love," and "hope" of the church. These words describe the total response of the believer to what God has done, is doing, and shall do.

Faith is not assent to a body of dogma. It is the stance of complete trust in God. The life of faith is also the life of love. One cannot be a believer without loving God and his brother. Hope describes the eager expectation and confident waiting of the believer for the future which God has promised to his children.

Paul wrote, therefore, about their "work of faith" or, better, the "work produced by faith." Their "faith [had] shown itself in action" (NEB). Significantly, he used the singular "work." The life of the believer is a unified whole. There is no division between secular and spiritual work. Everything that one does as a believer is done in faith and as an expression of faith.

In connection with love Paul used another word for work. Many of the versions translate it as "labor." It denotes exhausting, laborious toil. The emphasis is on sweat, discomfort, and hardship. The apostle did not describe the "labor prompted by love" (NIV). We may be sure, however, that it was work in and for the community, which expressed the love of believers for one another.

Hope expressed itself in steadfastness, endurance, perseverance. Christians in Thessalonica confidently believed that God was going to lead them into a glorious future. They showed how much they believed this by their steadfast endurance of all the persecution and hardships that their faith in Jesus Christ had produced.

The Success of the Mission in Thessalonica (1:4-7)

Paul was certain that the Thessalonian believers were among God's elect, "beloved" and "chosen" by him. He believed that it was impossible for people to respond to God if God had not previously taken the initiative by reaching out to them.

Paul was convinced that the labors of the missionaries had been in keeping with God's initiative in reaching out to the Thessalonians. They had not just spoken words, although Paul certainly did not depreciate the place of preaching in bringing conviction. God had affirmed their preaching by demonstrations of "power." Interpreters generally assume that power refers to miraculous manifestations of the presence of God, as in healing, for example. The Holy Spirit's presence had also been clearly discernible in the presentation of the gospel. Moreover, the three missionaries had preached with a "full conviction." This was in itself a manifestation of God's presence in their lives. So these three aspects of their ministry—power, the presence of the Holy Spirit, and great conviction—were evidence that they were within the will of God in the missionary work which had resulted in the birth of the church in Thessalonica.

Paul emphasized the way the gospel was presented to the Thessalonians. Next, he wrote about the way they had responded to it. They became "imitators" of the missionaries and "of the Lord." They responded to the authority of Paul's preaching and became followers of the Lord.

It had not been easy for the Thessalonians to respond to the preaching of the gospel. The society of the pagan city was hostile to such a stand. The "affliction" to which the letter refers is a special kind of suffering. The Greek word in the New Testament is often used to denote the suffering that one experiences because of his commitment to Jesus Christ. It is unjust and undeserved suffering.

But the Thessalonian Christians had not been negative and complaining. Indeed, the opposite was true. They had received the gospel with the "joy" that the Holy Spirit gives to believers. This combination of affliction and joy is characteristic of genuine believers.

The way the Thessalonians had received the word in the midst of great affliction made them "an example" for believers in the provinces of Macedonia and Achaia. Thessalonica was the leading city in Macedonia; Corinth was the principal city of Achaia. We must be careful not to interpret "example" in the wrong kind of way. We do not become Christians or act like Christians by following the example of anyone. We can only be Christian by the presence and power of God through our personal faith. The example of the Thessalonians bore witness to the divinely given realities of a life of faith. Such a course of conduct was possible to others who, inspired by the Thessalonians, also trusted God in the same way.

The News Spreads (1:8-10)

The news about the response of the Thessalonian believers to the gospel had spread rapidly. Indeed, it had preceded the arrival of the missionaries in other places. Instead of the missionaries themselves having to tell about what God had done in Thessalonica, they found other people already talking about it. "Everywhere" (v. 8) is hyperbole, of course. Paul meant "everywhere they had traveled."

The word translated "welcome" is translated in various ways that reflect the particular emphasis that the translators assumed to be correct. Among them are "visit" (NEB) and "what kind of reception you gave us" (NIV). Paul was primarily concerned about the result of the visit and not the personal welcome given to the missionaries.

And what had been the result of the visit? The readers had turned "from idols." This implies that they were pagans and not Jews. According to Acts, some Jews had responded favorably to the gospel (Acts 17:4). Most of the members, however, must have been Gentiles.

They had turned "to God." Paul could have stated that they had repented, for what he says corresponds exactly to the meaning of the word repentance. Repentance is a complete turning in the life, a radical change of direction.

This turning to God is further explained by the verb "to serve." The word literally means "to serve as a slave." The commitment to God is complete and unreserved. Of course it is voluntary commitment, a relationship into which believers enter joyfully and freely. In this way it differs significantly from the involuntary, grudging service of the slave.

The God of the Thessalonian believers differs from the pagan idols in that he is the "living and true God." God is the only one who can be described as living because he is the only one who is indestructible.

The last aspect of the change in the lives of the believers is that their values and goals are no longer defined by the things of this world. Their life has a greater and higher end. Thus, they expectantly await the coming of the Savior, God's "Son from heaven."

This hope is not mere wishful thinking. It is based upon what has already happened. God "raised" Jesus "from the dead." This means that he is alive. It also means that he has the power to deliver those who trust in him completely.

Paul taught that the salvation of the believer is complete. Jesus Christ deals with the problems of the past. He also meets the needs of the present. But what about the future? What will happen when God's "wrath" against sin is finally unleashed? Paul affirmed that Jesus can be trusted to deliver us in that eventuality also.

The Work of the Missionaries in Thessalonica

2:1-16

The Difficulties Confronted (2:1-2)

In the preceding verses Paul wrote about the glowing reports that had gone out from Thessalonica. In chapter 2 he turned to more specific comments about the ministry of the missionaries in that city.

The visit of Paul, Silvanus, and Timothy had not been "in vain"—that is, without results.

The missionaries' experience in Philippi prior to their arrival in Thessalonica had been such as to discourage further preaching of the gospel. In Acts 16:12-40 we read about the sufferings and humiliation endured in Philippi. Assaulted by a mob, beaten, and imprisoned, they had suffered both physical pain and emotional trauma.

The result of the persecution, however, was just the opposite of what might have been expected. The "opposition" in Thessalonica had been "great," but the missionaries had openly and courageously proclaimed the gospel. Paul described it as the "gospel of God," for he was well aware that such courage did not stem from human sources. It was "courage in our God" (that is, the result of their relationship with their God).

The Purity of Their Motives (2:3-5)

For some reason Paul was anxious to defend the purity of the missionaries' motives during their stay in Thessalonica. People in the Mediterranean world were accustomed to traveling philosophers, teachers, and religionists who exploited gullible people for their own gain. Also, perhaps the character of Paul and his companions had been impugned by their Jewish enemies in Thessalonica.

"Appeal" is a good translation of the verb in verse 3. Paul unashamedly preached for decision. Religion has always been a fertile field for demagogues who hide their real purpose behind their appeal. Paul's appeal, however, did not spring from "error." That is, he had not been the victim of false teaching. "Uncleanness" (RSV) is a literal translation. What is in view here is "impure motives" (TEV). "Guile" translates a word which means trickery or deceit.

Paul made a bold claim. He contended that the missionaries had been "approved by God." "Approved" translates a verb which means to find worthy through testing. God had tested the missionaries and had found them trustworthy for the responsible task of proclaiming the gospel.

Two of the main motivations behind the actions of many people are "greed" and the desire for "glory." Paul declared that neither of these had moved the missionaries. The Thessalonians themselves knew that, for they were aware that the missionaries had not sought to ingratiate themselves with their hearers by gratuitous "flattery." Even more importantly, God himself was a "witness" to the purity of the missionaries' motives. When Paul called upon God as a "witness," it was usually a sign that he was extremely serious about the point under discussion.

Gentle as a Nurse (2:6-8)

The Thessalonians might have expected Paul and his companions to exert their rights and authority as "apostles of Christ." After all, they were commissioned and sent out by the Lord himself, for this is what the phrase means. But they did not impose "demands" upon the new converts.

Instead of "[making] their weight felt" (NEB), the evangelists had been "gentle . . . [as] a nurse." The word means "wet nurse," referring to a woman who suckled a small baby. Since this was most often done by the mother, some versions have "mother" instead of "nurse." The main thing is to get the word picture of Paul's relationship to the Thessalonians. It was not characterized by authoritarian assertion of his desires but by the kind of gentle tenderness shown by a mother who nurses a small baby.

The great love which the missionaries grew to feel for their Thessalonian converts could be seen in their ministry in their city. Not only were they glad to share the gospel, but they were willing to share their "own selves."

The Unselfishness of Their Labor (2:9-12)

In verse 9 Paul elaborated on the way in which they had shared their lives with the Thessalonians. They had engaged in strenuous, difficult manual labor to support themselves so that they would not have to be a financial burden to any of the converts. Already traveling missionaries were accustomed to being housed and fed by the members of the congregation to which they ministered. Paul supported this practice, but he generally chose to support himself rather than depend on the churches.

To brave the sufferings and dangers experienced by Paul in Thessalonica in order to preach the gospel was certainly an expression of concern for the people. But at the same time to work hard physically, "night and day," to support themselves so they could share the gospel with their converts was an impressive proof of their affection.

Paul had used the metaphor of the wet nurse and the suckling child to describe his relationship with the believers. Now the metaphor changes because the idea is different. The wet nurse feeds the child.

The good father is concerned about the moral development of his children.

Moral problems were especially acute among believers newly won from paganism. They did not have the benefit of moral training like the Jews. Ignorance of Christian ethics, the pull of the old life, and the pressures of heathen society combined to hinder believers from leading lives worthy of the gospel. That is why so much of Paul's letter is given over to basic moral exhortation.

Paul believed that one of his basic responsibilities was to support new converts in their Christian life through exhortation and encouragement. The God who called believers to himself was a moral, holy, and righteous God. Conduct "worthy of God" was also righteous and moral. Goodness is a very important aspect of the Christian life.

High moral standards were in keeping with the high calling believers had received from God. God calls us to share in his "kingdom and glory." The kingdom of God is the sovereign rule of God. The glory of God is the manifestation of God as he really is. In the Bible the glory of God is often associated with light and dazzling brightness. Christians, therefore, are called to share eventually in God's own rule and nature.

The Acceptance of the Message (2:13-16)

The missionaries had been true, honorable, and loving in their ministry. For their part, the Thessalonian believers had been responsive to the proclamation of the gospel. So many of their neighbors had dismissed the missionaries' message as the "word of men." The believers could have responded in that way. But when the message was preached to them, the Thessalonian believers had been open and responsive to it. Their subsequent experience confirmed that it was indeed the "word of God," for it continued to be "at work" in them.

Previously Paul had said that the readers had experienced affliction when they received the word (1:6). At this point he let us know that the affliction was persecution by their own people. In this, their experience was similar to that of Jewish believers who had suffered at the hands of their countrymen. "Imitators" (v. 14) does not mean that the Thessalonians consciously imitated Jewish Christians. It simply means that their experiences were alike.

Notice the unusual designation "churches of God in Christ Jesus which are in Judea." This means that they were congregations of people who belonged to God by virtue of their relationship to Christ

Jesus. They happened to live in the province of Judea.

In this connection Paul opened the window somewhat on his own experiences as a Jewish Christian (vv. 15-16). He saw his persecution by fellow Jews as part of an age-old pattern of rebellion against God. They had killed the "Lord Jesus." Before that they had murdered the "prophets." They had driven Paul and his associates out. This may not refer to a specific incident but to a pattern of hostility, of which the persecution in Thessalonica was a part (Acts 17:5 ff.).

In Paul's case the reason for hostility was clear. He was "speaking to the Gentiles." His countrymen considered him a renegade, a traitor to his own people. The problem was not so much his theology as it was his insistence on the inclusion of the Gentiles in the church.

By their opposition to the gospel, unbelieving Jews were filling up the full "measure of their sins." This probably means that with this last manifestation of their rebellion against God their sin is complete. They had opposed God from start to finish, from the time of the prophets to the time of the preaching of the gospel to the Gentiles.

We cannot know what Paul meant by the last statement in verse 16. "God's wrath" in Paul's thought usually refers to the pouring out of his wrath at the end of this age. Here, however, it seems to refer to some occurrence or experience which Paul interpreted to mean that God's wrath had overtaken rebellious Jews at last.

The Mission of Timothy to Thessalonica

2:17 to 3:13

Paul's Desire to Visit the Church (2:17-20)

Acts tells us about intense Jewish hostility to the gospel in Thessalonica (17:1 ff.). The situation deteriorated to such an extent that the Thessalonian believers ushered the missionaries out of the city "by night" (17:10).

From Paul's comments about his departure we see how much he had wanted to stay. Evidently he feared that the Thessalonians were not strong enough in the faith to be able to confront the hostility to their new faith. He used a strong, vivid word to describe his forced separation from the new converts. The word literally means "orphaned." The RSV translates it "bereft"; "torn away" is even more forceful.

Paul was very anxious for his readers to know that his separation from them was not of his choosing. Although absent in body, he was never separated from them in his "heart." This means he had never ceased to think about them. Also, he had made every effort to visit them. His attempts were repeated, and they were not half-hearted, as the phrases "more eagerly" and "with great desire" bring out.

But Satan had thwarted Paul's efforts to return to Thessalonica. Sometimes Paul saw obstacles and problems as expressing the will of God (Rom. 1:13). In this case they expressed Satan's opposition to God.

How important were the Thessalonians to Paul? The apostle made every effort to let them know that they were absolutely indispensable. They were his "hope," "joy," and "crown of boasting before our Lord Jesus at his coming." "Coming" translates a special New Testament word, *parousia.* This word denoted the manifestation of a deity or the visit of a king or emperor. Early Christians chose it to refer to the coming of Jesus in power and glory at the end of the age.

When the Lord appeared, the Thessalonians would be there, as the fulfillment of the apostle's "hope." They would be his cause for rejoicing on that day. The "crown" is the victor's crown, the laurel wreath with which the winner of a race was crowned in the games. Paul's day of victory would be the day of the Lord's coming. The crown to which he would point with pride would be the believers won to faith through his ministry.

The Decision to Send Timothy (3:1-5)

Unable to make the desired visit to Thessalonica personally, Paul's anxiety about the new converts became unbearable. In this situation he decided to send Timothy back to visit them, even though it meant he had to remain in Athens without his trusted friend.

The reason for sending Timothy is made clear. The Thessalonians were under great pressure from their adversaries. Timothy was to perform the pastoral function of encouraging and exhorting the believers to remain true to Jesus Christ. Paul knew that the "lot" of believers was just such persecutions as the Thessalonians experienced.

In verse 5 Paul made it even clearer why his anxiety for the Thessalonians had become unbearable. He wanted to find out about their faith. This means that he wanted to find out if their trust in Jesus was of the quality that could stand up under persecution. He was aware of the power of the "tempter," here used as another name for Satan.

What is the temptation in the time of opposition and suffering? It comes from the sense that we have been abandoned by God. Or suffering can lead us to think that our trust is absurd. People who do not believe in God prosper while believers do not get along well.

Had the Thessalonians renounced their faith in the midst of persecution, the "labor" of the missionaries would have been "in vain." The word translated "labor" signifies costly effort. Perhaps "in vain" can be best understood as fruitless.

Timothy Returns with Good News (3:6-10)

Timothy returned bringing the kind of report from the church that the apostle had hoped to receive. Overjoyed by the word from the little band of besieged Christians, Paul decided to communicate with them by letter.

The "good news" brought by Timothy was twofold. He told Paul about the "faith and love" of the Christian community. These two qualities are often linked because one presupposes the other. The Thessalonians had really trusted in God. They had not abandoned that trust under pressure. But in Paul's theology, trust in God is always accompanied by love for our brothers.

Timothy also reported that the Thessalonians always remembered the missionaries with respect and love. They shared Paul's desire for a reunion.

As a preacher of the gospel in the first-century world, Paul experienced constant "distress and affliction." These words refer to spiritual anguish as well as physical suffering. The welcome news from Thessalonica was a source of encouragement in the midst of the pressures.

Verse 8 should be translated "since you are standing firm" (NIV). Relief from his oppressive anxiety about the Thessalonians is so great that Paul exclaims: "Now we really live" (TEV).

Paul could not find words adequate to express his overwhelming gratitude for the joy which filled his heart. He also pled with God to make it possible for him to return to Thessalonica. He felt that he needed to return to "supply what [was] lacking" in the church.

In none of Paul's letters do we get the idea that Christians in the churches had arrived at the zenith of their development. No matter what the progress, there was always room for further development.

Paul's Prayer (3:11-13)

Paul concluded the first major section of his letter with a prayer directed toward "God" the "Father" and the "Lord Jesus." In verse 12 he mentioned only the Lord. He could pray to God or to Jesus or, as here, to both. They were so identified that prayer to one was also prayer to the other. Paul, however, did not lose a sense of distinction between the two. The Father and Jesus were not exactly the same.

The apostle addressed three requests to God. First, he wanted God to clear the way for his visit to Thessalonica. Second, he wanted God to cause their love to overflow. Note that this love was not exclusive. It is expressed "to one another," to fellow believers, and "to all men," to nonbelievers. The love Paul wrote about is not primarily an emotion or a sentiment. It is a way of acting on another's behalf for his welfare.

Third, the apostle asked God to "establish" their "hearts." The heart is the center of intellect and will. What Paul was talking about is resolution and commitment. He wanted them to be strengthened in their dedication to a holy life—that is, one completely devoted to God. He mentioned the coming of Jesus because the hearts of men will be revealed then.

Paul believed that Jesus would appear one day "with all his saints." None of the Lord's people will be missing at the *parousia*.

An Appeal for Godly Living

4:1-12

Paul might well have ended his letter with chapter 3, for he had discussed the matters uppermost in his mind. Nevertheless, he added a second section to the letter which contains some ethical appeals and instructions. Some of the subjects probably were suggested by the report brought back from Thessalonica by Timothy.

Life Pleasing to God (4:1-2)

"Finally" in this case simply marks the transition to the exhortations found in the section. "Beseech and exhort" are synonymous terms which reinforce the seriousness and urgency of Paul's appeal. "In the Lord Jesus" describes the context of the appeal. Jesus was Lord of his life and theirs. Because of this, Paul dared to tell them how they "ought to live." "Live" translates a verb which means "walk" and has to do with behavior or conduct. What is important, of course, is that our conduct "please God."

Paul had been careful to give the Thessalonians instructions about Christian behavior. Diplomatically, he affirmed that the Thessalonians were indeed following those instructions. Yet there was room for development and growth. So he urged them "to do even more" (TEV).

Holiness in the Sexual Life (4:3-6a)

Gentile converts came from a pagan background characterized by very low moral standards. Sexual promiscuity, as well as other forms of immorality, was the way of life. Paul would not have written about these matters if they had not been a very real continuing problem in the Christian community.

He made it very plain in his letters that high moral standards were extremely important to the Christian life. What God wants is our "sanctification." His will is a holy life, not an immoral one.

If believers are to be holy, certain practices must be rejected. Among them is "unchastity." This word translates a term for general sexual immorality.

For a long time verse 4 has been the subject of debate. Probably, however, "vessel" should be understood as "wife" (RSV). There is yet another question. Were young men to "take" (RSV) wives in order not to fall victim to lust? I do not think that is the meaning of Paul's statement. Rather he urged men to learn how to live with their wives in a Christian marriage. Sex is an important part of marriage, but there should be a real difference between Christian and pagan marriage. In Christian marriage the wife is a person to be loved and not an object of lust. Sex in the context of love is holy and honorable. Otherwise, it is base and sinful. The "passion of lust" characterized the marriages of the "heathen" who did "not know God."

In his third injunction, Paul warned his readers not to "transgress, and wrong their brother." "In this matter" probably refers to sexual relations. In a word, they should respect their brother's marriage. The believer was not to take advantage of his brother's wife sexually.

A Solemn Warning (4:6b-8)

Paul gave three reasons why Christians should adhere to a life of moral purity. In the first place, the Thessalonians were reminded that the Lord punishes such offenses. The "Lord" is Jesus Christ seen in his role as Judge. Paul did not explain how sins of immorality would be punished, but he believed that judgment was a consequence of sin.

In the second place, Paul affirmed that believers were "called" into a life of "holiness" and not of immorality. The call referred to here is the call to become a member of God's people. It is the invitation sent out by God to accept the free offer of grace.

In the third place, when we are immoral, we are not "flouting" man but God (NEB). In this connection Paul mentioned the gift of the "Spirit" to the believers. The Spirit leads God's people to behave in ways that are pleasing to God. When Christians lead immoral lives, therefore, they are resisting the leading of the Spirit in their lives. Sin is an act of personal rebellion against God, committed in spite of all he does to prevent it.

Love for the Brethren (4:9-10)

In his exhortations to the churches Paul usually put love and unity in the community ahead of his call for personal morality. In this section he reversed the order and turned to the matter of love only after talking about the need for sexual purity.

We see another element in Paul's way of dealing with churches in these manners. Whenever possible, he began by emphasizing the positive characteristics of the readers. The Thessalonian believers were already distinguished by their "love of the brethren."

In the last part of verse 9 Paul changed to the usual word for "love" which flows from God. The Thessalonians had been "taught by God" to love their brothers. Love was a characteristic of the Thessalonian congregation from the very beginning. It was not something which Paul had found necessary to emphasize because a spontaneous loving attitude existed there already.

Their love was inclusive—they loved "all the brethren throughout Macedonia," the province of which Thessalonica was the principal city. We may be sure that their love was manifested in concrete ministry to the needs of other Christians. We get some notion of this spirit of Macedonian believers when we read 2 Corinthians 8:1-5.

Nevertheless, they could love "more and more." We have noted elsewhere that no Christian ever reaches the zenith in his spiritual life in this world. Each stage in our progress only prepares the way for the next.

Conduct in the Community (4:11-12)

Paul naturally moved from relationships in the church to the Christian's conduct and relationships in society. Our manner of life should be the kind that would earn respect from our unbelieving neighbors. Christians in the first century were often found in the center of trouble and disorder because of preaching the gospel. Paul himself had that experience. But he did not believe that they should get into trouble because of disorderly conduct, interfering in other people's business, or the failure to earn a living.

The Coming of the Lord

4:13 to 5:5

The Fate of Believers Who Had Died (4:13-18)

Apparently early Christians expected the Lord to return before they died. In Thessalonica some of the believers had already died. Evidently the church had some questions about this. What would happen to their brothers and sisters who were not alive when the Lord appeared?

In this passage Paul answered the question. He did not want his friends to "grieve as others do who have no hope." This does not mean that the believer will not be touched with sorrow. But it is a different kind of sorrow in that it is not the grief of despair.

For Paul the future of believers after death was tied intimately to the resurrection of Jesus Christ. Christians believed that God had raised Jesus from the dead. They needed to be confident also that the relationship of believers to God in Christ was not terminated by their own death. The physical death of Christians presented no problem to the God who brought Jesus back from the dead.

In verses 15-17 Paul described the scenario of the end time. The main point in the passage is his insistence that being alive at the return of the Lord will give no advantage to his readers. They will "not precede those who have fallen asleep." Three simple steps constitute Paul's vision of that wonderful day of the Lord. First, the Lord shall appear. Second, the "dead in Christ" will be raised. Third, all believers will be taken to "meet the Lord in the air." The word translated "meet" is a noun in the Greek text. It was a technical term for the public welcome accorded to important visitors by a city. Perhaps Paul was thinking about Christians giving Jesus a public welcome as their exalted Lord.

The "cry of command," the "archangel's call," and the "sound of the trumpet" were typical features of descriptions of the end found in Jewish literature of the period. It is impossible for us to know what the "cry of command" was. Who gave it? God, Jesus Christ, or the archangel? Was it God's command for Christ to appear? Or was it the archangel's command to the dead to arise? We cannot give dogmatic answers to these questions. But Paul wanted the Thessalonians to believe that physical death was no problem for believers. This was Paul's message of "comfort."

The Day of the Lord (5:1-5)

When is the Lord going to return? That question has been on the minds of believers over the centuries. Many people today spend a great deal of time with this same question. Paul told the Thessalonians that there was no need for him to write about this matter. "Times and seasons" refer to those decisive moments when God will act. Jesus also rejected such questions as improper because they dealt with matters "which the Father has fixed by his own authority" (Acts 1:7). The reason Paul gave for not writing about these matters is clear. He believed "that the day of the Lord will come like a thief in the night." This means that the return of the Lord will be totally unexpected. No need exists, therefore, to speculate about when it will occur.

The end will come when the people of the world least expect it. Just when they gloat in their own "security," the day of the Lord will arrive. Of course, that day has a totally different meaning for unbelievers than for believers. For unbelievers it will be a day of "sudden destruction." Its suddenness can be compared to the onslaught of labor pains experienced by a pregnant woman.

Believers do not have to be concerned about this, however, for they are already prepared. The day will be "like a thief in the night" only for the unprepared. But believers are not in "darkness." They are "sons of light." "Sons of" is a Hebraic expression which means "characterized by" or "belonging to." Believers are characterized "by light." They belong to the "day." Therefore, whenever the Lord appears, they are ready to meet him.

Final Admonitions

5:6-28

Spiritual Alertness Encouraged (5:6-11)

Paul pressed ahead with the application of his metaphor. People stay awake during the daytime. During the night people sleep and drunkards get drunk. Since his readers belong to the day, they are to stay spiritually "awake" and "sober." To be awake means that one is aware of God, alert to his opportunities, watchful against the attack of the enemy. "Sober" probably should be understood in the broad sense of self-control. It also speaks to a Christian's attitude toward alcoholic beverages.

The Christian soldier is to be alert. He is also to be armed. His armor is composed of those qualities and attitudes which the church already possessed and expressed in her life. They are faith, love, and hope (see comment on 1:3). Notice that "salvation" is the object of "hope." This is the typical Pauline way of thinking about salvation. It lay in the future, since it was the ultimate triumph of the believer over death and evil.

In a negative way, salvation for Paul meant that believers did not have to fear the "wrath" of God. They do not have to be in terror due to their anticipation of the judgment (NEB). The believer's destiny "through our Lord Jesus Christ" is salvation, which is deliverance from the wrath of God.

The relationship with Christ is not affected by death. He died and gained the victory over death. This means that our existence is bound to Christ's whether "we wake or sleep." These words are used by

Paul as synonyms for whether we live or die. He had already spoken of the dead as "those who have fallen asleep" (4:15). Some people have based a "soul-sleep" doctrine on expressions like these. According to them, the individual is simply asleep between his death and his resurrection. Paul, however, was simply using euphemisms, as we do, to speak about death. The main idea is the affirmation that death does not destroy our relationship with the Lord.

One of the great ministries of the church is the encouragement and building up of the weaker members of the body. Some people have more of a problem coping with the mystery of death and other matters which test our faith. The ministry of the church is to "encourage one another and build one another up" so that the weak will become stronger.

General Exhortations to the Congregation (5:12-28)

These verses give us one of those tantalizing peeks into the life of a young Gentile congregation in the first century. Obviously there was leadership in the congregation. How those leaders were chosen in Thessalonica we do not know. Paul did not use titles like pastors, elders, or bishops when he referred to them. They were those "over you in the Lord."

They derived their position and authority from their "labor." They were to be esteemed "because of their work" and not because of their office. One of the responsibilities of the leaders was to "admonish" the congregation.

The attitude of believers toward church leaders was respect "in love." From the very beginning churches have had problems in relating to their leadership. The solution to the problem is for people with responsible ministries to love the congregation and for the congregation in turn to love them. Then the ideal of peace that Paul wrote about is a reality.

The apostle specifically wrote about three groups in the church who needed special attention from the leaders. They were the "idlers," the "faint-hearted," and the "weak."

Problems with these groups intensified, as we learn from 2 Thessalonians. Idleness apparently grew out of a preoccupation with the *parousia*. If Christ were coming soon, some believers felt it was foolish to spend their time working.

The faint-hearted were the people who tended to become despondent over the death of loved ones and friends. In Romans (14:1) and

1 Corinthians (8:7) the weak had not completely thrown off the influence of their old pagan life. They were susceptible to returning to former practices. Perhaps this is what Paul meant in this epistle also.

"Patient" describes the genuine pastoral attitudes toward all these groups. Leaders are not to become exasperated and impatient with the imperfections and weaknesses of the congregation.

From his remarks about special groups Paul turned to the general needs of the congregation. Christians are not to respond to "evil with evil." Whatever the other person's actions or attitudes, God's people are always to do good. Joy, prayer, and thanksgiving are three related outstanding manifestations of the Christian life, according to Paul.

Verses 19-22 open another little window on the life of the church. In at least some of the churches the worship was informal and dynamic. Any member was free to deliver a message from God when he felt inspired by the Spirit. Paul was in favor of this practice, so he wrote: "Do not quench the Spirit."

Prophecy is not prediction. It is the proclamation of the inspired message from God given by the Spirit. Paul believed that prophecy was essential to the life of the church (1 Cor. 14). Perhaps some people had negative views about prophecy. They wanted more order and less spontaneity. So Paul wrote: "Do not despise prophesying."

Nevertheless, the hearers have a responsibility not to be gullible and accept every message just because the speaker claimed inspiration. The hearers were to "test everything."

A genuine message from God always leads people to do good. Believers were to "hold fast what is good." They were to "abstain from every form of evil," even if advocated in the name of the Spirit.

Holiness was of vital interest to Paul in this letter. He wanted the Thessalonians to live lives which expressed the reality of their relationship to God. At the end of the letter, therefore, he uttered a prayer for the holiness of the congregation. He believed that Christian living was the result of God's action in the believer's life. He was also confident that the goal of holiness would be achieved at the "coming of the Lord." This confidence grew out of his conviction that the God who had called (invited) them to himself would achieve the purpose of that call. God is "faithful." He can be trusted (NEB).

From his statement in verse 27, we see that Paul wrote his letter with the intention that it be read publicly in the worship of the church. This was the first step in the process that led to his letter being regarded as Holy Scripture.

2 THESSALONIANS

Introduction

After he had written his first letter to the Thessalonians, Paul received a report about problems and difficulties in the church. We do not know how the information reached him, for the second letter is silent on this question. Since the apostle was in Corinth, not too distant from Thessalonica, we may assume that there was occasional communication between him and the Thessalonians.

In an attempt to help the church with the difficulties about which he had heard, Paul wrote the letter which appears in our New Testament as 2 Thessalonians. From the contents of the epistle we can define the problems to which it was directed.

First, there was the matter of continued persecution to which the church was still subjected and which it apparently continued to meet with courage and faithfulness. Second, some person or persons had proclaimed to the church that the day of the Lord had already come. Apparently a letter purported to have come from Paul was being circulated in support of this view (2:2). Third, some members of the church were guilty of idleness and disorderly conduct.

Each of the three chapters in the letter deals with one of these problems. In chapter 1 Paul stressed the dire consequences that awaited the persecutors through the judgment of God. In chapter 2 he taught that the day of the Lord could not have arrived because certain events associated with it had not occurred. In chapter 3 he instructed the church to deal with its idle and disorderly members severely and yet in the Christian spirit of love and reconciliation.

The Justice of God
1:1-12

The Salutation (1:1-2)

The salutation is very similar to the one in Paul's first letter to the Thessalonians (see comment on 1 Thess. 1:1). We find two variations. Here God is called "our" Father. This established the basic relationship between Paul and the Thessalonians. If God is "our" Father, all who address him that way are brothers and sisters.

The source of the grace and peace for the readers is specifically mentioned here, whereas it is understood in the first letter. Grace and peace come from "God" who is "Father" and "Jesus Christ" who is Lord. Everything the believers received came from God because of their relationship to him through Christ. Thus either or both could be named as the source of the church's blessing.

Paul's Gratitude for the Believers (1:3-4)

Before he turned to the problems in the churches to which he wrote, Paul usually expressed thanksgiving for the good things in their lives. He does the same here, but with a different twist. He emphasized that he was "bound" to give thanks to God for the Thessalonians. "Bound" carries a sense of moral obligation. He also said that thanksgiving "is fitting." This stresses further the sense of moral obligation.

Why did Paul use these expressions? Some interpreters suggest that the Thessalonians had protested their unworthiness of Paul's praise in the previous letter (1 Thess. 1:2-3). Where "faith" and "love" existed in the church, however, it was wrong not to be grateful to God who was their source.

In the first letter Paul had written about the faith and love of the Thessalonians. The two go together in his thought because trust in Jesus Christ is always accompanied by love among believers. It is the evidence of the Spirit's presence in the church (Rom. 5:5).

"Growing" faith and "increasing" love called forth thanksgiving in this letter. Faith and love are not static. They are dynamic. We never trust or love as much as is possible. So we need to be concerned not only about their presence but also about their increase.

Paul did not mention hope here as he did in the first letter (1:3). He did speak about the evidence of hope, which was "steadfastness" and "faith" in "persecutions" and "afflictions." "Steadfastness" describes the victorious stance of believers who continue to trust God in the face of opposition. The persecutions which the Thessalonians had confronted at the beginning (1 Thess. 1:6) still continued. But they had not wavered in their commitment to God.

Righteous Judgment (1:5-10)

It is difficult to determine exactly what Paul considered to be "evidence of the righteous judgment of God." Perhaps the proof that God is going to judge righteously is the "steadfastness" of the Thessalonians. This was the result of God's presence in the church. The power of God in the life of the believers was proof that they would emerge victorious. Evil had not prevailed. The enemy could not accomplish his purpose. This was evidence of the weakness of the forces opposed to God. Steadfastness in persecution meant that God would count the Thessalonians "worthy" to share in his "kingdom" (that is, in his victorious rule).

Vindication of the persecuted is one aspect of the righteousness of God's judgment. The other aspect is the punishment that will be meted out to the persecutors. The believers were under great stress and strain at the moment. Their suffering was called "affliction." This word translates a key Pauline term which denotes the suffering experienced for the sake of the gospel. It is not just any kind of suffering. It is suffering for the "kingdom" (v. 5). God would grant them relief. The word used to indicate relief originally meant the release of the tension on a bow string. Here it signifies release from suffering for the gospel.

Paul included himself with the Thessalonians when he spoke of this relief. He also was under constant stress for the gospel. The appearing of Jesus Christ is spoken of as "the Lord Jesus [Christ] is revealed from heaven." Christians know Jesus as Lord now. But at his appearing his lordship and authority will be revealed to all. He will be seen as he is. Jesus will be revealed "in flaming fire." This imagery is taken from the Old Testament where God's appearance is associated with fire (Isa. 66:15, for example). Fire is a symbol of the glory and might of the Lord, and perhaps of his judgment.

The people who are objects of God's wrath are those who "refuse to acknowledge God" (NEB). Also they do not "obey the gospel," which means "they do not accept the good news." When he made these remarks, Paul was thinking specifically about the persecutors of the church. Their hostility to the gospel was the evidence of their rebellion against God.

The righteous judgment of God will be "eternal destruction" for the enemies of the gospel. The phrase implies a belief that their state of destruction is never-ending, although the word translated "eternal" can also have other meanings. Paul did not elaborate on the nature of the destruction except to say that it meant "exclusion from the presence of God." Eternal separation from God was paramount in his mind with all that it meant.

On the other hand, the "saints" or believers would enter into full relationship with him and inherit the glories of the kingdom. The exact meaning of the last part of verse 10 is not clear. The preposition can be translated "in" (RSV) or "among" (NEB). In the first instance, the glory of God will be beheld in what he does "in his saints." If you ask "Who will marvel?" the answer may be the angelic hosts. They will see how great God really is when he saves his people. In the second instance, the saints themselves will glorify God and marvel at him when they experience the reality of their full salvation.

The Thessalonians could be sure that they would be in that number because they believed the "testimony" of the missionaries. The testimony was their witness to the gospel. What separated the lost and the saved in Thessalonica, therefore, was the response of individuals to the proclamation of the gospel.

Paul's Prayer for the Thessalonians (1:11-12)

Paul was always conscious that the future of believers was totally dependent on God. Therefore, it is not contradictory for him to assure his readers that God would count them worthy and at the same time constantly pray to God that he would do so.

"Every good resolve and work of faith" probably should be understood as the resolve and work of the believers. Both resolve and action are essential in the life of holiness. Good resolves need to be carried out in work that expresses confidence in God. God is the one, however, who fulfills the resolve and gives the energy for the work of faith. The result is that we cannot take credit either for our good purposes or for carrying them out in action.

With the fulfillment of good purpose in work of faith, "the name of our Lord Jesus may be glorified" in his people. Name stands for the person in the biblical context. The name of Jesus is "Lord." When our lives are lived in keeping with his purposes, he is shown to be our Lord and, thus, receives the glory that is due him. Those who glorify the Lord will also be glorified in him. Our glory is to be God's people. We can rest assured that God will own us as his people in Jesus Christ—that is, because of our relationship of living for and belonging to him.

The Day of the Lord
2:1-17

We now face one of the most difficult and problematical passages for the interpreter in Paul's letters. For one thing, the passage is uncharacteristic of Paul. In his other letters Paul does not attempt to give this kind of detailed description of the events of the end time. For this reason some scholars believe that he did not write 2 Thessalonians.

We may assume that both Paul and his readers had some idea of who the characters and what the events in this drama of the end time were. The guesses by interpreters as to their identity have been many and varied. The only conclusion which we can reach with assurance is that the exact meaning is shrouded in mystery for us.

The Problem (2:1-2)

Paul's teaching about the end time was directed at a problem in the Thessalonian congregation. Evidently someone had told them that "the day of the Lord" had already come. Clearly the "coming of the Lord" and the "assembling" of the saints to meet him (1 Thess. 4:17) had not yet occurred. But the "day of the Lord" could refer to the whole series of events connected with and preceding the coming of the Lord.

We may guess that the Thessalonians had been told that certain events had already transpired which meant that the second coming of the Lord was about to take place. As a result, the believers were "shaken in mind" or "excited." "Excited" translates the same verb found in Mark 13:7. There the problem also was that the disciples could misinterpret certain developments as an indication that the end had come. According to Mark, Jesus told them: "Do not be alarmed." The purpose of the two passages, therefore, is the same.

Paul wrote in order to calm the church and help its members to keep their minds on their personal responsibility for faithful Christian living. Belief that the end was at hand could lead to irresponsibility and excesses. Paul did not want the Thessalonians to give credence to wrong teachings about the end, whether they came "by spirit or by word, or by letter purporting" to come from Paul himself. "Spirit" refers to a revelation claimed to be given by the Spirit. "Word" refers to an oral proclamation. Possibly a letter also had appeared in Thessalonica attributed to Paul himself which put the apostle's authority behind the erroneous teaching.

The Events of the End Time (2:3-12)

The point in Paul's message to his readers is clear. The day of the Lord could not have come because the events associated with it had not taken place.

What Paul saw as the events of the end is fairly easy to see. How they should be understood is the difficulty—a difficulty we cannot resolve with the knowledge we have.

One of those events is the "rebellion." A Jewish tradition spoke of apostasy from God and the law at the end time. Paul apparently adopted this idea. But how did he understand it? Many people have applied it to Christians who would rebel against God and give themselves over to unrestrained evil. The main problem is that Paul does not teach elsewhere that believers will become apostate. The opposite is true. In passage after passage he affirms his confidence that God will bring believers through all affliction to achieve his purpose of glorifying them (Rom. 8:29-30,38-39).

Associated with the rebellion is a personage, evidently historical, whom Paul called "the man of lawlessness." He is also called "the son of perdition," a Semitic expression which means "man doomed to destruction" (NEB).

This lawless one is further described. He "exalts himself" against every so-called god or object of worship. Paul recognized idolatry as evil. But the lawless one represented the epitome of idolatry in that he exceeded all else in his claims for man's worship.

He also "takes his seat in the temple of God." This means that he occupies God's own throne, which is brought out by the explanatory phrase "proclaiming himself to be God." The problem is about how we are to understand "temple." Is it the Jerusalem Temple still standing at the time? The word for "temple" means the "sanctuary," the center of Israel's worship. It was the place where God was enthroned in the midst of Israel.

For Paul, however, the Temple no longer had the significance given to it by other Jews. The true temple of God was the church (1 Cor. 3:16). From the fourth century the predominant view has interpreted the temple as the church. In the past the lawless one has been identified by some as the pope. Many other identifications have been offered.

Another figure is introduced in verse 6. One problem is that "what is restraining" is in the neuter gender in the first instance, and "he" who restrains is masculine in the second (v. 7). Do these refer to the same thing? That is, is the person (v. 7) an expression of the power (v. 6)? There is no satisfactory answer. Many different interpretations have been offered. Some people have identified the restraining power as the Roman empire. Others have suggested that it is the gospel and that Paul as a preacher of the gospel is the person who restrains.

One thing is fairly obvious. Paul believed that the power of evil was at work even then. But he called it the "mystery of lawlessness." This means that the lawless one is at work in a hidden kind of way—incognito, as it were. But this lawless power was limited temporarily by an opposing power which acted as a restraint.

The time would come when the restraint would be removed. Then the "lawless one will be revealed." This means that he will be seen as he really is. He will appear in his own person. His coming will be accompanied by "power and with pretended signs and wonders."

The lawless one is also pictured as a deceiver. He uses his mighty works to lead people astray. In other places in the Bible we read of the danger of accepting miracles as the proof of the activity of God (Matt. 7:22). People who are deceived are also called those who "refused to love the truth." The acceptance of the truth of the gospel through trust in Jesus Christ is the believer's protection against deception.

The revelation of the lawless one will be the signal for the "appearing" of Jesus the Lord. The authority and power of the Lord is greater than his. The Lord will slay him by the "breath of his mouth." Even in Revelation, where the crisis of the end is depicted as a battle, the weapon of the Lord is his word (Rev. 19:15). Also, Paul wrote, the Lord will "destroy him by his appearing." That is, the coming of the Lord is sufficient to overcome the lawless one.

Verses 11-12 present problems for many of us. God is given responsibility for the "delusion" of those who "perish." Let us note, however, that primary responsibility for their fate is charged to the unbelievers themselves. They "refused" the truth by which they could be saved. They preferred to be deluded.

Paul taught in Romans (1:24 ff.) that a process can be seen in the lives of people who reject God. He believed that this process was an expression of the wrath of God. When men reject God and follow idols, they begin a process of spiritual deterioration. They go downhill in terms of spiritual degradation. In the passage here, the refusal of the truth is the responsibility of those who worship the lawless one. A part of the penalty for their sin is a spirit of delusion. This is the opposite of the Spirit of God, who leads into an ever-deepening perception of reality. The spirit of delusion is the penalty of rebellion.

The end result is that the destruction of the false god means condemnation also for his worshipers. He was destined for destruction, and he pulls down to ruin all who follow him.

Although Paul did not use the term, possibly the lawless one should be identified as the Antichrist. We are left, however, without being sure of this and without knowing who he is.

Chosen for Salvation (2:13-17)

This passage is related closely to the preceding one but is marked by a shift in thought. Paul spoke about the fate of unbelievers in the previous verses. In these he wrote about the future of believers. The passage illustrates a point we made in the difficult passage above. Whatever he meant by the "rebellion" (v. 3), clearly he did not expect the Thessalonians to fall away from God. As always, his confidence about the future of the church was rooted in his faith in God. The readers were "beloved [of God]," a phrase that belongs to the category of election. It singles them out as the people whom God chose "from the beginning to be saved." Two ideas are paramount. The relationship of believers to God is possible only because God takes the initiative. Apart from his choosing and calling, salvation is not possible. In other words, our salvation depends totally on God. Furthermore, "to be saved" points to the future, a characteristic of Paul.

The present life of believers is described by "sanctification" and by "belief in the truth." "Sanctification" is the ongoing process of growth through the direction and power of the Spirit, who is leading believers to become what God intends them to be. "Belief in the truth" is not assent to a body of doctrine. The truth is personal; in a word, it is Christ. Belief in the truth is expressed by trust in him.

At the beginning of the Christian pilgrimage is the call "through" the gospel. At the end is the "glory of our Lord Jesus Christ" which believers will share. Between those two the Spirit works for our sanctification. As Christians wait for their glorification, they are to "stand firm." The Thessalonians were not to be shaken or excited (2:2) by false teachings or discouraged by persecution. They were to be guided by the "traditions" delivered to them by Paul. "Traditions" translates a technical term meaning that which is handed down. Paul used it to refer to the common teachings of the Christian community that had been passed on from the beginning.

The activity of the "Lord Jesus Christ" and "God our Father" is closely linked in Paul's thought. Paul could confidently call on God to help his readers because he "loved" them. The love of God was expressed concretely in the gift of the Savior and in his death on the cross. His grace is also seen in the provisions made for his people in their present struggle. Those provisions are "comfort" and "hope." They are closely linked, of course. God does comfort his own now by his presence and encouragement. A part of that comfort is also the wonderful expectation of future redemption from the sufferings experienced in an evil world.

God is asked to "comfort" and "establish" ("encourage and strengthen"—NIV) the church in every "good work and word." This means that Christians are not just to await their future redemption passively. God encourages them so that they can be actively involved in the good work of faith and in the proclamation of the gospel.

Final Exhortation
3:1-18

Paul's Request for Prayer (3:1-5)

The apostle prayed for believers. He also felt a need for their prayers on his behalf. We cannot but be struck by the difference between his prayers and those of Christians today. He expressed no concern for things like health, material prosperity, or good fortune. His interest was focused entirely on his role as a minister of the gospel.

In this regard, he was concerned about two matters. First and foremost, he was interested in the spread of the gospel. "The word of the Lord" is the redemptive message about Jesus Christ. His desire was that it spread swiftly and that it meet with the proper response. "Triumph" is literally "be glorified" (KJV). Men honor or glorify the gospel when they acknowledge the lordship of Christ.

Paul knew, however, that some people would reject the gospel and harass its messengers. Therefore, he asked for deliverance from those "wicked and evil" people who did not respond in faith.

People are often unfaithful or rebellious against God. But there was one sure comfort in the face of their hostility. The "Lord is always faithful." He can be trusted to care for his own. In this connection, Paul's thoughts turned again to his readers, who were under severe pressure. God would "strengthen" them. This was their bulwark or guard against evil. In Greek no noun follows "evil." Paul was thinking about evil people (TEV) or Satan. God does not deliver his own by taking them out of tough situations. He gives them the strength to stand up for their faith.

Paul's optimism about the Thessalonians was rooted, as always, in his "confidence in the Lord." Two of the ways in which the Lord provides for the needs of his people are mentioned. He prayed that the "hearts" of his readers be directed toward the "love of God." This can mean God's love in their hearts for one another. In the context it probably should be understood as God's love for them. The knowledge that God loves us brings strength. "The steadfastness of Christ" can be that which Christ gives. Probably it means that Christ's steadfastness is an example for Christian living. In the face of the harshest cruelty, Christ never faltered.

The Problem of the Idlers (3:6-15)

In 1 Thessalonians we saw hints of a specific problem in the church (5:14). It had become serious enough to compel Paul to deal with it severely. A group in the church, probably not large, refused to work. The apostle felt that the church needed to take stern measures to correct it. Therefore, he instructed the church to "keep away from any brother who was living in idleness."

Note that even here he calls the erring person "brother." Later on in the passage it becomes clear that his advice to the church was designed to help the "brother" adopt a more Christian life-style.

Paul had taught the Thessalonians that they should work. He called this instruction "tradition." This identifies it as a commonly accepted teaching in the churches. Moreover, the apostle cited the example set by the missionaries while they were in Thessalonica. They had supported themselves so that they "might not burden any of you." Paul believed that the preacher of the gospel had a "right" to support from the congregation (Gal. 6:6). But Silas, Timothy, and he had not availed themselves of that right.

In verse 10 Paul repeated the specific instruction given to the Thessalonians. We must be careful to keep one point in mind. The early church felt a specific responsibility to care for the needy. We should not use this passage, therefore, to justify lack of Christian compassion. Nevertheless, Paul believed and taught by word and example that believers were to be responsible members of society.

The people condemned by Paul were not only idlers; they were also "busybodies." They used their time to stir up trouble. The Christian community was instructed not to feed such people and so contribute to their sin. Hospitality was a Christian virtue prized by Paul and practiced in the early church. But such fellowship was not to be extended to the idlers and busybodies.

Paul certainly assumed that the problem members would receive his message, for he addressed himself directly to them in the letter (v. 12). His instructions were simple and clear. He expected them to "lead orderly lives" (TEV). The problem was not that they were loud in their work. They were troublemakers. The letter further enjoined them to "earn their own living."

The church was not to be hostile and treat the problem member like an "enemy." He was still a "brother" for whom Christ had died, but one who needed to change his ways. The church had a responsibility to "warn him as a brother" (that is, in a spirit of love and with a desire to help him). The purpose of Paul's instruction, therefore, was clearly redemptive.

Concluding Remarks (3:16-18)

The conclusion to the letter contains some typical remarks. Paul was always concerned about peace in the church as an expression of the members' relationship with their Lord. Since Jesus was the Lord of peace, peace in the church was evidence that they were under his authority. Peace is a gift to be accepted and not the product of human achievement. Paul usually ended his letters with a prayer for "grace." The total existence of the church—past, present, and future—depended on the unmerited favor of God.

Verse 17 is an unusual comment. Paul dictated his letters. Probably he did not write well, not unusual in those times. Evidently his handwriting was distinctive, easily recognized. He adopted the practice of writing the closing greeting in his own hand. Paul told the church that this was the "mark"—that is, the evidence of authenticity—in every letter written by him. Perhaps the reason for this was to guard against forgery. We have seen a hint in this letter that the Thessalonians themselves had received a forged letter (2:2).

1 TIMOTHY

Introduction

First Timothy belongs to a special group of Pauline letters which we call the Pastoral Epistles. They contain advice on how to order the life of the churches.

Timothy

Two of the Pastorals are addressed to Timothy, one of the most intimate associates of Paul. He was a native of Lystra, a city visited by the apostle on his first missionary journey. According to Acts, he was the son of a Gentile (Greek) father and a Jewish mother (16:1). He joined Paul and Silas (Silvanus) on the second missionary journey (Acts 16:1-4). From that time the younger man was a constant companion of the apostle, as attested by the account in Acts and the references to him in many of the Pauline letters.

The Occasion of the Epistle

Paul and Timothy had spent some time in Ephesus. Finding it necessary to travel to Macedonia, the apostle had requested that his associate remain in Ephesus to help the churches with their organization and doctrine.

This task was all the more urgent because the churches were experiencing difficulties from heretical teachings. We cannot define the heresy clearly, but certain aspects of it emerge in the epistle. It evidently embraced Christian, Jewish, and pagan ideas and was wildly speculative in nature (1:4). The Jewish law was one of the ingredients in the mix of ideas (1:7–11). There was also an emphasis upon asceticism. Hostility to marriage and prohibition against eating certain foods (4:3) were aspects of the heresy. It was promoted as a means of acquiring knowledge (6:20), which was probably the same as salvation.

Place and Date

According to 1 Timothy, the letter was probably written from Macedonia. But we cannot fit the notice of 1 Timothy 1:3 into the details of Paul's life given in Acts or the letters. One way conservative interpreters have dealt with the problem is by a hypothetical reconstruction of Paul's life after his imprisonment in Rome. According to the hypothesis, Paul was released from prison at that time (around AD 63) and returned to the region of his former missionary endeavors. He was subsequently arrested, imprisoned, and executed around AD 67. This hypothesis places the events of 1 Timothy during the time of freedom between the two imprisonments.

The Salutation

1:1-2

In the address of his letters Paul followed the form of first-century letter writing. Three of the elements in that form give the structure to the opening of 1 Timothy. They are the name of the writer, the name of the recipient, and a greeting.

When Paul called himself an "apostle" in the salutation of his letters, he was often underlining his authority. Apostle meant "one who is sent" and could refer in a general way to a messenger or emissary. Paul used the term, however, in a special sense. He equated his call and his role in the churches with that of the original apostles, such as Peter, James, and John. His apostleship was based upon the fact that he, like them, had been called and commissioned directly by Jesus Christ for a special ministry.

He served as an apostle under the lordship of "Christ Jesus." The origin of his apostolic ministry was God himself. It was at the "command of God" that he had committed himself to the service of Christ.

Timothy was one of the close associates of Paul in his missionary labors. He had enlisted Timothy on the second missionary journey (Acts 16:1-3). Timothy had served with Paul "as a son with a father" (Phil. 2:22). Perhaps this is the relationship the writer had in mind when he called Timothy "my true child in the faith." The statement may also imply that Paul won Timothy to faith in Christ.

Paul added "mercy" to "grace" and "peace," which are usually the two terms found in his greetings. Mercy is a virtual synonym of grace. Grace is the love of God which causes him to act on their behalf without regard to their merits. It is the basis of their relationship into which believers have entered because of God's grace. They have been reconciled to God and to one another. Peace exists, as God's continuing gift, where once alienation and hostility reigned.

The Threat to the Gospel
1:3-11

In our study of early Christian history, we observe one fact which has been verified over and over again in later times. The first challenge to the gospel is the hostility and rebellion of the pagan world. Soon after the gospel is preached, however, another threat arises. This time it comes from within the ranks of those who call themselves believers. Invariably there are interpretations of the gospel or additions to it that threaten to change its nature so that it becomes something quite different from what God intended. That seems to have happened in all the churches which God brought into being through Paul's preaching.

Much of Paul's energy was devoted to evangelism. Much of it, however, was also devoted to developing the fruits of his evangelistic efforts. Especially was he taxed in mind and spirit to protect his churches from the inroads of false teachings.

The Threat from False Teaching (1:3-6)

For reasons that he does not explain, Paul found it necessary to leave Ephesus to go to Macedonia. Those reasons must have been imperative to take Paul away from a church that was unsettled by conflicting ideas being spread among its members. The apostle did the next best thing possible to deal with the problems. He left his valued and trusted companion, Timothy, in Ephesus to deal with the problems.

Paul had "urged" Timothy to remain at Ephesus. Was the urgent insistence due to his reluctance to remain behind? Possibly so. But it may have been due to Paul's deep concern about the welfare of the church. The reason for his insistence that Timothy remain behind is stated immediately. There were some people in Ephesus who were teaching a "different doctrine." There are several references to this heretical teaching in the letter, but its nature does not emerge clearly. It was evidently a mixture of the Christian gospel with elements foreign to it and contrary to its nature. The result was a perverted Christianity.

These false teachers occupied themselves "with myths and endless genealogies." There is strong disagreement among scholars as to the exact nature and source of these speculations. The basis of it was probably Jewish. It was a way of interpreting the Old Testament. This was done through fanciful stories or legends and interpretations of genealogical passages like those found in Genesis. Interpreters probably found hidden meanings and revelations in those passages. Fanciful legends and speculative interpretations were very common in early Christian heresies.

The test by which this approach is proved to be wrong is the result which stems from it. They "promote speculations" or "controversies" (NIV). Every generation has seen its share of teachers who major on the kind of biblical study which divides rather than unites believers.

At the center of God's revelation is not a myth or legend. It is an event—the event of the incarnation, death, and resurrection of the Jesus Christ. The great truths of that revelation are simple and clear, although not easy to accept and live by. An emphasis on the truth of the gospel brings believers together; it does not divide them into warring camps, each defending its own interpretation of obscure passages.

As Paul put it, the gospel promotes "divine training that is in faith." The word translated "training" is one that we might translate in other contexts as "stewardship" or "plan." Indeed, other versions translate the phrase here as "God's plan, which is known by faith" (TEV; also see the NEB). Whether the word means training or plan, the key is faith. The truth of God is contained in an event to which we respond in faith.

The purpose to which true Christian instruction or preaching leads is a life of love (v. 5). The supreme test of any interpretation of the gospel, therefore, is this: Does it lead its hearers to love God and each other?

The love that the New Testament talks about is a special kind. It is not a response to what is lovely or lovable in the other person. It arises out of our nature as redeemed children of God and goes out to people without regard for their personal merit.

This love, according to our text, "issues from a pure heart and a good conscience and sincere faith." In the Bible the heart is the center of the inner life of man—his emotions, intellect, and will. According to the gospel, God transforms man at his very center. The person thus transformed may be said to have a pure heart. He is committed to the service of God from the center of his being. A good conscience is the practical equivalent of a pure heart. The person with a good conscience is not condemned by the memory of attitudes and actions which express rebellion against God.

All of this is related to "sincere faith." A person cannot have a pure heart unless he has really trusted God. Evidently Paul was contrasting this with what the false teachers called faith but was not the real thing. They were enamoured with their own wild speculations and did not trust solely in God's grace. They had left that which was genuine to become wrapped up in "discussions" which were empty and futile.

A Wrong Understanding of the Law (1:7-11)

The Jewish character of the heretical teachings is seen clearly in this section. The teachers claimed to be teachers of the law and made dogmatic assertions about it.

Evidently they applied the law in the wrong way because they misunderstood its purpose. Perhaps they made the keeping of the law—as interpreted by them—the standard of the Christian life. The purpose of the law was not to save but to expose the sins of people who were rebels against God—that is, the "lawless and disobedient" (vv. 9-10). The function of the law was to condemn and not to save, to judge and not to vindicate. The false teachers were using the law *unlawfully* and perverting its true function in God's plan.

If they had understood the law aright, they would have seen that they themselves were under its judgment, for their teachings were "contrary to sound doctrine." The criterion by which all teaching was to be judged was the "glorious gospel" itself (v. 11). If any interpretation of Scripture or understanding of the will of God perverts the gospel, the center of our faith, it is to be rejected. The gospel is the good news that God has acted to save men in Christ, apart from the law.

Paul's Praise of God's Grace
1:12-20

This passage is a kind of parenthesis, an outburst of praise for the grace of God. It was motivated by the closing thought in verse 11. The gospel had been committed to Paul as a trust. He felt responsible for preserving its genuine character. Paul not only wanted people to trust Christ; he cared for them after they became Christians. He was responsible for the gospel. This meant that he also had the pastoral duty of helping people to understand it and remain true to it.

But when he thought of how God had trusted him, he was overwhelmed by the knowledge that this trust was undeserved. This moved him to express his deep gratitude to God.

For Being Placed in Christ's Service (1:12-14)

Three attitudes characteristic of Paul's view of his ministry are expressed in verse 12. First, Christ himself was the source of his "strength." Paul would take no personal credit for any of his accomplishments. If he had been able to do anything at all, it was only because of God's power working through him.

Second, being a servant of Jesus Christ was a privilege beyond comprehension. Paul never did feel that he was making a sacrifice by serving Christ. Quite the contrary! He considered it a blessing which he did not deserve.

Third, when Christ calls a person into his service, his doing so implies trust. It is an act of faith on the part of Christ, as incredible as that may sound. Paul felt great responsibility for living up to that trust.

We cannot understand the meaning of grace for Paul unless we realize that it came out of the experience described here. Christ had not saved and trusted Paul because of his past record. He had "blasphemed and persecuted and insulted" the Lord. The only explanation for his present relationship to Christ was grace, completely undeserved love.

Paul does say, "I had acted ignorantly in unbelief." This statement was not made to excuse his rebellion in any way. No doubt, he had in mind the false teachers of Ephesus. Their rebellion against God could not be attributed to their lack of knowledge of the gospel. It is one thing for an unsaved sinner to rebel against his Lord. It is quite another for a person who claims to be a believer to sin perversely against him.

For Making Him an Example for Other Sinners (1:15-17)

At the heart of these verses is a saying that seems to have been widely expressed in the Christian communities: "Christ Jesus came into the world to save sinners." This statement expresses the very heart of the gospel. In the person of Jesus of Nazareth, God had become incarnate. The purpose of that incarnation was to save sinners like Paul. God's purpose is universal. It reaches out to all people. Once an individual sees this, he cannot isolate himself from God's purpose. Like Paul, he is compelled to be an instrument through which God's redeeming love can reach out to the sinners for whom it is intended.

Paul knew from personal experience that this truth was "sure." The word translated "sure" means "reliable, worthy of full confidence." God had saved Paul, even though he was ranked first among all sinners.

This affirmation is not made because Paul wanted to appear excessively humble. He made it because he wanted people to know that the God who had saved him could save anybody.

The contemplation of the incredible redeeming grace of God caused Paul to break out into a doxology. The God whom Paul praised is "the King of ages." This means that his rule is universal and eternal. He is "the only God." Christians, like Jews, were monotheists. They believed that there was only one God. The relationship between Father, Son, and Spirit was understood in a way that did not lead them to believe in three Gods.

The Charge to Timothy (1:18-20)

If Timothy were to perform the task assigned to him, it was necessary for him to make sure of his personal commitment to the gospel. The pressures of the environment present constant danger to the Christian minister. It is so easy for him to adapt his life and message to fit the current trends. Paul was aware of the danger and concerned that Timothy not yield to it.

Timothy was to remember "prophetic utterances" which had led

Paul to perceive the promise of a very young man. These "prophetic utterances" were the inspired declarations of others about Timothy's spiritual possibilities and future contributions to the gospel. We can only guess at their content, but we have heard many such utterances about promising young people as they entered the ministry.

Timothy was not to be false to those optimistic pronouncements. "Inspired by them," he was to "wage the good warfare." The Christian life is a struggle. There are always adversaries. Paul was fond of using military metaphors to describe this struggle. The weapons in this spiritual struggle are "faith and a good conscience." Trust in Jesus Christ, the one who redeems and strengthens, is central. A good conscience stems from an awareness that one is living this life of faith.

A bad conscience arises when one says he knows God but denies it with his life. There were some vivid examples of this kind of error, of people whose lives contradicted their profession. Perhaps they had started out well, but they had ended in "shipwreck." Two of these people, Hymenaeus and Alexander, are named.

There is a parallel to verse 20 in 1 Corinthians 5:5. To deliver "to Satan" probably means at least exclusion from the church. The two men had been put outside the community of faith where Christ reigns. They had been put back into that sphere where Satan rules. The purpose, however, seems to be redemptive. The writer hoped that this severe measure would cause them to "learn not to blaspheme." Blasphemy in this instance probably meant to pervert God's truth.

Instructions for the Church

2:1-15

The basic concern in the pastorals is for the order of the church. There are injunctions governing individual morality and conduct, but these always are viewed in the perspective of the relationship of the person to the redeemed community. The individual Christian is never viewed in isolation. He is always understood as a part of the whole. Indeed, this is true of the entire New Testament, but it is more explicit in the Pastorals.

In the passages considered in this section, the writer is talking specifically about the congregation as it meets for worship. The instructions are intended to guide the church in the conduct of its meetings.

The Scope of Public Prayer (2:1-7)

The church has a role as intercessor, not only for those in its fellowship but also for everybody outside the community. It is not to allow its concern for people expressed in its prayers to be limited by any of the world's superficial categories of race and class. It is to pray "for all men."

Four different words for prayer are used by the writer, of which the one translated "prayers" is the most general. Not only is prayer to be made for all; every kind of prayer is to be made for them.

The writer singled out one group for special emphasis. They were "kings, and all who are in high positions." Judaism had established a pattern which early Christians followed. Jews prayed for government officials. Until the outbreak of the Jewish-Roman War (AD 66-70), sacrifices for the emperor were made in the temple.

There were times in the early Christian experience when the state became the persecutor of the church. In the book of Revelation, for example, the state, personified in the emperor, is viewed as the Antichrist. For the most part, however, during that early period, the rulers of the empire guaranteed a stable situation which was a benefit to the gospel. A positive attitude toward governing officials is expressed here, as well as in Romans 13 and 1 Peter 2.

A prayer in the spirit of that enjoined here is found in 1 Clement, written about AD 96: "Give them, O Lord, health, peace, concord, and stability, that they may exercise without offence the rule thou hast intrusted to them." It is clear what Paul hoped to be the outcome of intercession for rulers. It is expressed in the clause "that we may live a quiet and peaceable life." Christians can hope and pray that government will guarantee the stability and freedom in which they can serve their God.

But some might object to Christian prayer on behalf of pagans, who were enemies of God if not of the church. The writer grounded his injunction, therefore, in a belief that was central to his theology. Although men may live in active rebellion against him, God's purpose for the pagans is the same as that for believers. He desires "all men to be saved." This does not mean that all will be saved. But if they are lost, it is in spite of God's redemptive purpose.

Belief in one God led Paul inevitably to the belief that God's purpose embraced all mankind. Furthermore, there is "one mediator." In the religious world of the time people believed that there were many angelic mediators between God and man. Paul believed, however, that God had come to mankind in one person and in one alone.

Jesus had given himself as a "ransom." A ransom was, for example, the price paid to secure the freedom of a slave. In the New Testament there are two major points of emphasis. First, there is the emphasis on what it cost to secure our liberation. Jesus "gave himself"; he died on a cross. Second, there is the fact of the liberation itself. What Jesus secured was our freedom. These ideas are brought out clearly in the NEB translation: "who sacrificed himself to win freedom for all mankind."

In the context of this letter, of course, the emphasis is on the phrase "for all" (that is, "for all mankind"). This was Paul's point. If Jesus died to save all, Christians certainly are right in praying for all.

Paul himself is an example of the working out of God's universal purpose. By divine appointment he was a "preacher and apostle . . . , a teacher of the Gentiles." Through him God was reaching out to that pagan world whom his fellow Jews had excluded from the covenant community.

Paul experienced great criticism and persecution from Jews because of his ministry to Gentiles. They did not believe him when he said that God had called him to preach to Gentiles. For this reason we find the protest in verse 7: "I am telling the truth, I am not lying."

Instructions for Men and Women (2:8-15)

Public prayer is the subject in verse 8. "Place" probably had become a somewhat technical term for place of worship. In the early church this was usually the home of some believer. By implication the men were to do the public praying.

A common Jewish posture in prayer was evidently widely adopted by early Christians. While they stood, they looked upward toward heaven, lifting their arms with the palms turned upward. This may have symbolized the expectation of receiving God's blessings in answer to their petitions. Of course, the posture in prayer is not sacred, and various postures are found in Scripture.

The main point is character and attitude. The lifted hands are "holy" if the person has genuinely committed himself to God. Basically, "holy" means belonging to God. Also the believer's attitude toward other people is important in prayer. We are to pray "without anger."

The right kind of prayer cannot be offered if we are out of fellowship with our brothers and sisters.

The instructions for women in the Pastoral Epistles create problems for Christians today. In practice, if not in theory, we have recognized that some aspects of these teachings are provisional. For example, dress codes vary from place to place and from time to time. What is modest and sensible is different in different cultures. Also, we permit women to teach, conduct public worship, and pray in the assembly. This seems to imply our belief that practices vary from one time to another.

Underlying the instructions in the Pastorals, however, are certain fundamental principles which never vary. Believers are to be concerned about order in the church. Furthermore, they are to so live and behave that they do not bring reproach on the gospel or become a stumbling block to nonbelievers. The Christian faith should issue in a Christian life-style. Christian principles should be made concrete in the varying conditions and in the various cultures in which God's people live.

The first point had to do with the way women were to dress when they attended the public worship of the church. Modesty rather than ostentation was to be the governing principle. The worship service is not the place for a style show. The injunctions about dress reflect the fact that the church membership was still largely made up of the lower classes. Most of the members could not afford the kinds of things prohibited by the writer.

Styles and customs change. What is unacceptable in one era or in a certain situation may be acceptable in another. But Christian concerns should still be determinative for the Christian community. We should be concerned about our Christian relationship with less fortunate brothers and sisters. The way we dress does make a statement about such things.

The main concern for Christians, then as now, should be character and not dress. As Paul put it, there needs to be a close and coherent relationship between behavior and belief, between deeds and profession.

The exact role of women in the early church is not clear. It seemed to vary to a great extent as reflected in the New Testament documents. In Acts 18:26 Priscilla and Aquila both taught Apollos the "way of God." Since she is mentioned first, Priscilla was evidently more important in the early church than her husband. In 1 Corinthians 11:5

Paul gave instructions for women who pray and prophesy (preach) in the church.

According to the passage in 1 Timothy, women were to "learn in silence." They were not permitted to teach or to exercise any leadership role in the church that would give them authority over men. In Genesis Paul found two ideas to support his position. Man was created before woman. Furthermore, the woman was "deceived" by the serpent. The idea seems to be that women are by nature more vulnerable to deceptive and wrong ideas than are men. The writer believed that they should be learners, therefore, and not teachers—that is, not teachers of men.

Verse 15 contains a rather difficult statement. The RSV translates: "Woman will be saved through bearing children." We should note that the writer does make it clear that "faith and love and holiness" are more crucial than childbearing.

Of course, most non-Catholics reject the idea that childbearing has anything to do with personal salvation. The point in 1 Timothy seems to be this: Childbirth is a God-given role which women perform. When they bear children, they are fulfilling their role as women. When they transgress, they are rebels against God. When they function as mothers, they are doing what God intended in creation. In this they are distinctive from men. Plainly put, the writer believed that men were destined by God to be teachers; women were created to be mothers.

The Qualifications of Officers
3:1-13

There seems to be no doubt that development took place in the organization of the church from the time of Paul's earlier epistles to the Pastorals. In passages such as 1 Corinthians 12:4-10 and Romans 12:6-8, the situation in the church seems to have been much more fluid and less organized than that reflected in the Pastorals. We note, however, that Paul specifically addressed only the bishops and deacons when he wrote to the Philippians (1:1).

Certain truths appear to be clear. There is no single pattern of church order reflected in the New Testament. Furthermore, no church was organized in the same way that churches are organized today. Indeed, we cannot say with assurance just how the churches were organized in New Testament times.

Moreover, the important point to remember is that the church should function as the body of Christ. The nature of the church is constant; the forms of its life vary in order to fulfill that nature. The authenticity of the church is found not in its organization but in how well it fulfills the purpose of its Lord.

Bishops (3:1-7)

The word "bishop" means "overseer." The bishop in the early church seems to have been called elder also. The meaning of the word indicates that the bishop had administrative responsibilities in the church. This is borne out by the statement found in verse 5.

In addition to his administrative tasks, the bishop also needed the qualifications of the teacher. Men chosen as bishops are also to be "apt teachers" (v. 2). Bishops played a significant role, therefore, in helping to maintain the doctrinal health of the churches. Perhaps it is significant that nothing is mentioned which would lead us to believe that the bishop was to function as an evangelist or a prophet.

Today in our church life the pastor fills the roles of administrator, teacher, shepherd of the flock, preacher, and evangelist. There is no New Testament passage where all these gifts are attributed to any one officer of the church.

Two aspects of the bishop's calling are apparent in our passage. First, it seems to be assumed that the individual himself "aspires to the office of bishop." The writer made it clear that such an inspiration is a good thing. In fact he emphasized this, which indicates that there may have been negative attitudes toward those who expressed a desire to be bishops.

Second, the church has responsibility for selecting its leaders on the basis of their qualifications for the office. This means that no one is to be chosen just because he wants the job or even just because he believes that God has called him to be a bishop.

In our churches we emphasize these two aspects of the call to ministry. The individual must have a sense of his own calling. The church, however, must also have a conviction that he is the one who can fulfill the responsibilities of the office. The Pastoral Epistles do not talk of this in a mystical kind of way. Not feelings but specific character-istics are to guide in the selection of the church leader.

The first emphasis is on the personal moral qualifications of the bishop. Various adjectives are used. The exact sense of some of them is hard to pin down, as can be ascertained by looking at them in various translations. The general picture, however, is clear enough. The bishop is to be morally above reproach. He is to be characterized by moderation and self-control. He is not to be given to vices, such as drink or greed. He is to be gentle and peaceable in his relations with other people.

One qualification calls for specific comment. The bishop is to be "the husband of one wife." We cannot be dogmatic about the sense of this injunction. It can mean, for example, that he is not to be a polygamist. The need for such a rule would stem from the fact that men who had married two or more women as pagans subsequently were converted and became members of the church. Probably, how-ever, the statement means that the bishop is not to have more than one living wife. He is not to be a divorced person.

Another qualification for the bishop is that he must "manage his own household well." He is to be respected and obeyed by his children. The presupposition is that a person who cannot be a bishop to his own family can hardly qualify to be the bishop of the church.

Furthermore, the bishop is to be an experienced Christian, not a new convert. The reason given is that a rapid rise to prominence in the church could lead to pride. The devil's sin was pride. The person guilty of this sin will "fall into the condemnation of the devil." Two possible interpretations of this may be seen in versions other than the RSV. According to the TEV, the conceited person will "be con-demned, as the Devil was." In the NEB the condemnation is "con-trived by the devil."

Last of all, the bishop should have a good reputation in the commu-nity outside the church. It is essential that he not be the object of reproach or "scandal" (NEB) in the pagan community. The word for "devil" also means "slanderer" and could be translated in this way in verse 7. The bishop's life could make him a victim of gossipers. But we are probably right in translating "devil." The person whose actions make him an object of "reproach" in the pagan community has fallen into a snare set for him by the devil.

Deacons (3:8-13)

The word translated "deacons" literally means "servants." The word was used for people who served tables. By the time of the Pastorals it had come to be used of a specific group of people in the church who played a helping role in its life.

It is clear that the helping role of deacons places them in a position of church leadership. Extreme care is to be given, therefore, in the selection of these men. They are to be "serious"—that is, people whose character engenders respect. This certainly does not rule out the expression of Christian joy.

Furthermore, deacons are not to be dishonest, addicted to alcohol, or materialistic. Also, they are to be committed personally to the "mystery of the faith." This phrase is best understood to mean the "truths of our faith" (NEB). For Christians these truths were no esoteric mystery. Indeed, in the closing verses of this chapter Paul set forth the basic truths to which believers are to be committed. A "clear conscience" is the result of knowing that one honestly and genuinely holds to these truths and lives by them.

Deacons are not to be chosen hurriedly or thoughtlessly. The text says: "Let them also be tested first." It is not clear what the process of testing is to be, but it is clear that candidates are to undergo close scrutiny.

The family life of the deacon is important. The word translated "women" in verse 11 also means "wives" and probably should be so understood in this context. The character of the wives is to be taken into consideration in the selection of deacons. The wives are to be "serious," respectable, of good character. They are not to indulge in destructive comments about other people. They are to be "temperate" and "faithful," trustworthy, in all situations. The word "temperate" can refer specifically to the use of alcoholic beverages, but it also can have a much wider application.

Like the bishop, the deacon is to be the "husband of one wife." Once again, we cannot be absolutely sure about the meaning of the phrase. As we noted earlier (3:2), it probably means that he is to have only one living wife. The stress, however, is not on the legal aspect but on the devotion of the deacon as husband. He is to "be faithful to his one wife" (NEB).

Also like the bishops, deacons should "manage their children and household well." The reason, however, is different. In their leadership of their family and its affairs, bishops prove their competence to be overseers of God's household. The main idea with regard to deacons seems to be their standing in the Christian community. If their family life is good, they will enjoy the respect of their fellow Christians.

Two results stem from the good service of deacons. First, they receive the esteem of others. They "gain a good standing for themselves." Second, those who serve well will gain "great confidence" in the faith. It is not clear how we should understand the second part of verse 13. The "great confidence" mentioned by the writer may be the deacons' own personal assurance about their faith. But it also can refer to the boldness or confidence with which they can speak about their faith. The word translated "confidence" can mean the boldness to speak openly or publicly.

The Minister's Task in Difficult Times
3:14 to 4:16

The Truth of the Gospel (3:14-16)

If Paul had been personally able to deal with the problems in the churches, we would not have the letters which make up such an important part of our New Testament. The letters were substitutes for a personal visit, as the writer stated here.

His concern was behavior in the church. The word translated "household" literally means "house" (KJV). In the New Testament, however, the church was not a building. Rather, it was the people. The idea was that of the "household" or family. Paul was interested in the relationships of people in that family, not the way people behaved in a building. He set forth principles to guide those relationships. It is also apparent that "church" here has a broader connotation than just the local church in Ephesus. It is the people of the living God, wherever they may be found.

The church has a special responsibility for the truth. Paul spoke the "pillar and bulwark of the truth." That truth was under attack by people who were involved in wild speculations.

The word "mystery" here, as we have noted, is to be understood as revealed truth. It is not primarily concepts; it is truth revealed in an event. It is certainly not found in the myths and genealogies of the false teachers. As we have said, Christian truth is expressed in the central event of our faith—the event of the incarnation.

Several aspects of this truth are expressed in the confession of faith given here. We probably should understand this as a confession or a hymn used liturgically in the churches. This means that it was not composed by the writer of this epistle.

The first truth is the reality of the incarnation. God came into the world as a human being known as Jesus of Nazareth. Moreover, he was "vindicated in [or by] the Spirit." The verb translated "vindicated" means "declared righteous." The reference is probably to the resurrection which was by the power of the Spirit and through which Jesus was shown to be the righteous Son of God.

The phrase "seen by angels" is perplexing. The basic idea seems to be that the authority of Christ was manifested to angelic powers. They were all subordinated to him. This was an important concept in the first century when so many people believed that their lives were controlled by principalities and authorities—by heavenly or angelic powers associated with the stars.

The significance of the incarnation is worldwide. By preaching the gospel "among the nations" the early missionaries were true to the redemptive purpose of God. That preaching had borne fruit, for Christ was "believed on in the world." Faith in this present age is the appropriate response to the preaching of the gospel.

Finally, he was "taken up in glory." Perhaps this is placed last because the hope of the believer to be received into glory is based upon the confidence that he has been preceded by his Lord.

False Teachings (4:1-5)

The Christian faith was preached, accepted, and lived out in a world where there were many ideas that threatened it. There is always a tendency for the gospel to be adapted to its environment.

In early Christian history there was a set of ideas which we commonly call Gnostic (word derived from a Greek term meaning "knowledge"). Basically these ideas arose from the conception that only that which was spirit was good; matter was evil. When these concepts permeated Christian thought, they gave rise to many different lifestyles. One of these was prevalent in the area to which our writer directed his attention. People taught that every effort should be made by believers to dissociate themselves from the material world of flesh. Primarily this meant that they were to abstain from marriage and not eat certain kinds of foods. Generally the forbidden foods were wine and meat.

The writer was not surprised that some church members were attracted by these ideas. New Testament prophets under the inspiration of the Spirit had foretold that just such an abandonment of the faith would occur in "later times." Later times may also be translated "last times." New Testament writers as a whole seem to have believed that they were living in the last times.

There is no question but that the writer was alarmed by the heretical doctrines. They are demonic in origin rather than coming from the Spirit of God. Those who taught them are called hypocritical "liars."

Paul said that the consciences of the false teachers were "seared." The teachers were insensitive to the difference between truth and falsehood. The verb translated "are seared" may also be rendered "is branded" (NEB). If we accept this translation, the statement means that they bore the brand of Satan, "the devil's sign" (NEB). They belonged to the devil.

The false teachers demanded celibacy and abstinence from foods. The author believed this was a grave error. We have seen that he instructed Timothy to select married men as bishops and deacons. In another context Paul taught that it would be better for some people not to marry (1 Cor. 7:26-27). But even there the counsel was prompted by the circumstances of the Christian and the demands of the gospel. Paul did not teach anywhere that marriage is evil.

He also rejected any division of foods into those which were good and those which were evil. He went back to the Genesis account to support his position. Whatever exists was created by God. Everything God made is "good," by the witness of the very Word of God. Therefore, nothing created by God is to be rejected for food because it is evil.

How is the Christian to relate to the things God created for food? First of all, he is to receive them "with thanksgiving." The believer knows the "truth"; he knows that what he eats was created by God for his good. He also knows that it is a gift and, therefore, to be accepted with gratitude.

Food that the Christian eats is "consecrated" or made holy by the "word of God and prayer." Perhaps "word of God" is a reference to the Genesis account of creation (see Gen. 1:12, for example). "Prayer," of course, would be the blessing of the food in which the believer who partakes of it gives thanks.

The Good Minister (4:6-10)

We cannot be sure about the translation of the word for "minister." In Greek it is *diakonos.* We translate it "deacon" if it refers to the special group of helpers in the church (3:8). Literally, the word means "servant" and perhaps should be so understood here (NEB).

What are the characteristics of the "good minister [servant] of Christ Jesus"? He is faithful in laying before other believers those "instructions" which will enable them to avoid the dangerous teachings to which the writer has referred. Moreover, he will be concerned about the quality of his own personal life. He is "nourished" on the true teachings of the gospel. The word translated "nourished" is a present participle. It indicates that Timothy was to feed daily on the teachings of the "faith" and the "good doctrine" which had guided him to this point in his life.

This is the positive side. The negative is also important. Believers are to avoid those things which are harmful. Paul had already referred to the "godless and silly myths" (1:4). He called them godless because the false teachers presented them as the truths of God. They evidently served as the basis for prohibitions against marriage and against eating certain foods.

Paul emphasized the need for personal discipline in the life of the Christian minister. He is to "train [himself] in godliness." The NEB emphasized the present tense of the imperative: "Keep yourself in training for the practice of religion."

The metaphor is lifted from the realm of athletic activity. As the athlete disciplines himself and exercises to be able to compete in the games, so the believer must stay in training spiritually. The training in godliness, however, is much more important. The discipline of the athlete has "some value," but it is limited to the welfare of this physical body. Our physical bodies, however, are doomed to death no matter how much we exercise. By contrast the things of God are relevant both to the present life and the life to come.

One thing is clear from this passage. Being a good Christian is not limited to what we say we believe but is concerned above all with the way we live. There is to be a definite relation between belief and behavior. Another truth is also apparent. We do not become good Christians by accident but by rigorous and consistent discipline in living.

The faithful saying referred to in verse 9 is probably the reference to training in godliness found in verse 8. In other words, Paul quoted a saying which was probably current in the Christian community.

The arduous nature of the Christian life is underscored by the verbs "toil and strive" in verse 10. "Toil" translates a word describing hard, physical labor. "Strive" was used for the great effort expended by athletes in wrestling, for example. They are good words, therefore, to describe the effort involved in living godly lives.

The athlete strives to achieve a goal—the laurel wreath of the victor. The believer also strives because he has a goal in mind: eternal life. His hope for this life is set on God. Paul described him as the "living God" because he possesses and bestows the only life that is of value.

The universal note which we encountered in 2:1-7 is sounded again. God is the "Savior of all men." "Savior" here points to God as the ultimate Deliverer from sin and death. God stands ready to deliver all. He is the only hope that people have. Paul evidently found it necessary to sound this note because some people believed that certain groups stood outside the scope of God's redemptive purpose. God is the potential Savior of all. He is the effective Savior, however, of "those who believe." The only barrier to salvation lies in men. There is none in God's love and purpose.

The Example of the Minister (4:11-16)

We do not know how old Timothy would have been at this time. Anyone under the age of forty could be considered a youth. We have to remember that there was a special reverence for age during that time. The church evidently tended, at least on occasion, to fail to show proper respect for leaders who were considered youthful. From the point of view expressed in the letter, respect was not to be predicated on age.

The members of the church were not to "despise" Timothy's "youth." This means that they were not to dismiss his leadership and counsel because they felt that he lacked the wisdom of age. Respect was commanded by the quality of life. So Paul enjoined Timothy to "set the believers an example" by what he said, the way he lived, his teaching of the major Christian virtues of love and faith, and the morality of his personal life. The responsibility for receiving respect, therefore, lies with the Christian leader. He cannot expect it if his life does not merit it.

Verse 13 sets forth three of the major responsibilities of the minister in public worship. From the earliest days, following the pattern of the synagogue, the reading of passages from the Old Testament was an integral part of public worship. In those times many of the church members were illiterate, which made the public reading all the more important. As time went on, Christian churches also included the reading of things such as Paul's letters and the gospels in their public assemblies. In this way the New Testament canon grew and began to occupy a place alongside the Old Testament.

"Preaching," which included exhortations as well as revelations from the Spirit, also was an important part of Christian worship. Teaching those matters essential for Christian thought and living was carried on from the beginning.

The "gift" referred to in verse 14 is Timothy's endowment for ministry. The word gift emphasizes the truth that his capacity for ministry was not a personal achievement. It began as something received from God. The minister, nevertheless, has a responsibility for cultivating and developing his gift, a responsibility that has not always been recognized.

The fact that Timothy had been endowed by God for ministry was recognized at the beginning by people inspired by the Spirit. Through their "prophetic utterance" they had publicly declared that God had endowed him for his special work. This had been confirmed by the laying on of hands by the presbytery, the "council of elders." The ministry of any individual, therefore, is to be understood and appreciated in the context of the church. The church in one way or another recognizes that God has endowed a person for ministry and affirms its solidarity with and support of his ministry. A "Lone Ranger" type of ministry is a denial of the New Testament concept. It teaches that the ministry of individuals has significance only as part of the ministry of the whole body.

If the promise of the beginning was to be realized, Timothy had to devote himself to the disciplined "practice" of the ministry. One thing is clear in verses 15 and 16. The minister does not begin fully developed. Apparent "progress" should be seen in his personal life and in his work as a minister.

The last part of verse 16 presents a theological problem. We need

to remember that the word "save" had various connotations in the
New Testament. Basically the Greek word meant "deliver from danger or disease." In theological language it could mean the initial deliverance of the believer from sin. Often, especially for Paul, it meant
the ultimate triumph over death and the entrance into glory.

The word, however, could also have a present connotation. We
are being saved. God is active in our lives, continually redeeming
and delivering us. In this passage the writer was probably thinking
of the perils which confronted Christians in his day. If Timothy were
faithful to the teachings of the gospel, he would be saved along with
his hearers from the dangers of the false teachings which threatened
the church.

Duties Toward Others

5:1 to 6:2*a*

Relationships with Various Groups (5:1-2)

There are many metaphors for the church in the New Testament.
One of the most meaningful is that of the family of God. How is
the younger minister to relate to various age groups in his church?
The writer takes his cue from the relationships in the family.

The position of the minister makes him subject to special kinds of
temptations. He may be arrogant, abusive, arbitrary, and unloving.
Paul was aware of this, and his counsel was designed to prevent those
attitudes unbecoming to a Christian minister. The minister has the
responsibility of addressing himself to the problems, sins, and needs
of people of all ages. He must be careful, however, that he does so
in the right spirit.

When he addresses an older man, the minister is not to be "harsh"
(NEB). He must give spiritual counsel, but it is not to be in the nature
of a "rebuke." Rather, it is to be an appeal, as though he were addressing his "father." He is to treat "older women like mothers."

Younger men are to be addressed as his "brothers"; younger women,
as his "sisters." The spirit with which one preaches to or advises people
makes all the difference in the world. It has been rightly said that

the preacher can say anything he wants to his congregation if they are sure that he loves them.

Responsibility Toward Widows (5:3-16)

The criterion for widowhood (5:3-8).—From the very first, churches recognized and accepted the responsibility of caring for the unfortunate among their membership. Two of the major groups of needy people were widows and orphans.

Most of us pay only lip service to the principle that Christian love is to be expressed in terms of concrete help for the disadvantaged. Always, however, when we move to put into effect programs for helping the poor, we are confronted with many practical problems.

One problem is the financial limitations of any church. Any person or group of people can only do so much. Another problem is that of determining whether people are genuinely in need of help. These are the kinds of practical matters which lie behind the instructions found in this section of 1 Timothy.

In those days the churches generally were poor. They were very limited in the amount of disposable goods available to help their needy. Therefore, they had to discharge their responsibility in a very sensible way.

"Honor" in verse 3 means to give material help. This was one of the main ways, for example, that Jews could show that they truly honored their parents (see Mark 7:9-13). "Real widows" designated the women who were considered the responsibility of the church. No widow was to be classified for the purpose of receiving help if she had "children or grandchildren." It seems to be assumed that these family members were Christians. If so, they were to carry out their "religious duty" by caring for their own. In a very real sense they owed a debt to the parents and grandparents who cared for them when they were helpless. They had an opportunity to pay that debt when one of their own became a widow. That is the idea in the phrase translated "make some return to their parents" (see NEB).

The "real widow" is one "left all alone" in the world. But this is not the only criterion laid down by Paul. The widow is to be a dedicated Christian who "has set her hope on God." The "supplications and prayers" of the widows probably should be understood in terms of the life of the congregation. One role that these elderly widows could play in the church was that of constant intercession and prayer. These prayers probably referred to those made in the daily assembly of the congregation (see NEB). This was their ministry in the church.

The opposite of this ministry of prayer is the life of self-indulgence or pleasure. A widow, supported by the church, could use her idle time in seeking self-gratification. Paul was aware of this possibility and felt that steps should be taken to guard against it. Apparently widows supported by the church were to function in a sense as full-time ministers of the church. Their time was to be spent in the ministry of prayer and not in the seeking of pleasure.

What does it mean to be a Christian? For some the answer is found in emotional, spiritual, other-worldly terms. For the writer of the Pastorals, being a Christian is expressed in the most concrete way. At the center of what it means to be a Christian is the responsibility of providing material support for the helpless members of one's own family.

A person may be orthodox in his doctrinal expression, involved in the corporate life of the church, and pray long prayers. But if he fails to care for the widows of his family, he has, by that very neglect, "disowned the faith." Moreover, he is "worse than an unbeliever." Here the idea seems to be that many people who are not believers perform these elementary acts of love. A Christian who does not care for needy widows is worse than an unbeliever who does so.

The eligible widows (5:9-16).—The writer had stressed the point that the widows who are to be supported by the church and give full time to its ministry must be "real widows." Now he gave other limitations, all of them practical in nature. Those who were to be enrolled were to be at least "sixty years of age." This reflected a need to cut down the number of such persons dependent on the church. Moreover, they were to be women who were married only once. They should have a proven record of "good deeds."

The qualification of having "brought up children" provokes a question. The real widow had no surviving children. Perhaps what is meant here is that the eligible widow was one who had cared for orphans. "Hospitality" was an important Christian virtue in the early church. When other Christians, especially traveling teachers and preachers, visited the church, they had to be entertained in the local homes.

When guests arrived for a visit, it was the custom to wash the dirt of travel from their feet. This was a task normally performed by a slave if the family owned one. The widows, therefore, were to have demonstrated their humility and willingness to serve by washing the "feet of the saints." "Saints" in the New Testament means believers.

Another qualification was the ministry of love for the "afflicted." This would include the sick and others in distress. By the acts of ministry listed here, the widow demonstrated that she had the qualifications to be a minister of the church.

"Younger widows" were to be rejected. The reason for this was that they might grow "wanton against Christ." The idea seems to be that their desire to marry would make them turn away from their commitment to serve Christ as widows. Their "first pledge" refers to their original dedication to serve Christ as widows in the church.

Visitation was apparently an aspect of the ministry of widows. There is always the danger that people involved in church visitation will indulge in gossip and meddling. The writer seemed to believe that younger widows would be more inclined to this kind of thing than the older ones.

Younger widows, therefore, were enjoined to remarry and fulfill the functions of a wife and mother. By so doing, they would not furnish an occasion for slander against the church. It is not clear if "the enemy" (v. 14) is Satan or a person. Probably the idea is that he is a person who is the instrument of Satan.

Verse 15 apparently gives the reason for the precautions set forth by the writer. "Some have already strayed after Satan." They had already done the very things that Paul was concerned about. Some who had dedicated themselves to Christ had remarried. Others had created problems for the church by being "gossips and busybodies."

It is difficult to know why the writer thought younger widows would be more inclined to gossip than older ones. Perhaps he felt that the character of the older women would be better known to the church. Gossip is certainly not confined to any age or sex.

There is a textual problem in verse 16. The RSV adopts the readings of some good manuscripts in its translation "believing woman." The point of the verse, however, is clear. "Relatives" should assume responsibility for the widows in their families. This would free the churches to use their meager resources for the widows who were left completely alone in the world.

Instructions Concerning Elders (5:17-25)

The support of elders (5:17-18).—There are various passages in the New Testament which show that material support was provided for some ministers from the very beginning. When Jesus sent out his disciples on their mission, he made them dependent upon the people who were recipients of their ministry (Mark 6:7-11; see also Gal. 6:6). Here the matter is carried a step further. Not only are ministers worthy of support, but some should receive more than others.

"Elder" and "bishop" evidently are synonymous terms. Elder is the more Jewish term, and bishop is the more Greek concept. The leaders of the Jewish community were often referred to as elders. This stems from the fact that they generally were the older men of the community.

An elder who showed himself proficient in leadership was "worthy of double honor." "Honor" here means pay, financial remuneration, as it often does in the Jewish context. Simply stated, this means that the best leader should get twice as much.

Special consideration was to be given to those who also labored in "preaching and teaching." The ministry of the word was the highest of all. This passage shows that the function of administrator was not always combined with that of preaching, as it generally is in our churches today.

Instructions about sinning elders (5:19-22).—Any public person is vulnerable to slanderous, false accusations. Paul was aware of this. His instructions have the double purpose of safeguarding the church leader and the congregation. No charge against an elder was to be accepted unless there was evidence to substantiate it. According to Jewish law, "two or three witnesses" were the minimum number necessary for conviction in a court of law. All of us have known pastors and other ministers who have been the tragic victims of innuendo, gossip, and unfounded accusations. The church has a grave responsibility to protect the reputation of its good ministers from this kind of assault.

Unfortunately, however, church leaders often succumb to temptation and sin. Paul felt that these situations called for remedial action. In the RSV we read that such action is to be taken against elders who "persist in sin." This phrase is the translation of a Greek present participle. It brings out the force of the present tense, which is "to continue in," "to persist in." It is the stubborn refusal to give up a sin which calls for corrective action.

There are two aspects to the discipline. The "rebuke" is to be administered publicly, before the whole congregation. It must be administered without "partiality." Evenhandedness should characterize the discipline of the church.

All of this leads to a concluding admonition. Men should not be ordained as elders hastily. It is true that we cannot predict the future conduct of any person. The only thing the church can do is to examine the person in the light of what is known about him. The cause of Christ has suffered greatly because people obviously unfit for the ministry have been ordained. Churches suffer in many cases because they do not take time to really find out about the known character of the persons they call as their ministers. If one participates in the hasty ordination of a minister, he has some responsibility for the tragedy which often follows.

Concluding remarks (5:23-25).—Into this section Paul inserted a prescription for Timothy. He was advised to "use a little wine" for his stomach's sake. This may imply that Timothy suffered from some kind of stomach ailment. Wine was widely used for medicinal purposes in the first century.

The statements in verses 24-25 may be connected with the foregoing discussion of possible sins of the elders. We know that there is a lot of evil hidden from public scrutiny. Also, there is a lot of good that goes unnoticed. But Paul did not believe that evil could remain hidden forever in God's order. Nor did he believe that goodness would be covered up ultimately.

The church has a responsibility for the moral quality of its leadership. That responsibility is limited, however, because our knowledge of the good and evil in other people is limited. Eventually all will be apparent. We may be sure of this, for God, the only Judge, knows our hearts.

Instructions for Slaves (6:1-2*a*)

In the New Testament no voice is raised against slavery as an institution. The tiny Christian minority had no power to change the evil institutions of a pagan society. Apparently the number of slaves greatly outnumbered slave owners in the membership of the churches.

The focus of attention, therefore, was on how the Christian slave could make a positive contribution to the welfare of the gospel. Slaves were urged to honor their masters. The concern was for the "name of God" and for the Christian "teaching" or message. The writer felt that a rebellious slave would bring discredit to the gospel from the pagan world. The slave represented his God and his faith under very difficult circumstances.

Some few slaves could have masters who were also members of the church. This raised special problems. How should slaves regard their responsibility to such masters? Possibly the slave in this situation could take advantage of the relationship, refusing to carry out his master's commands. However, the writer taught that the opposite should be true. Their service should even be superior. After all, the beneficiaries of their service were not unbelieving pagans but members of the community of faith and love.

Conclusion

6:2*b*-21

The Motives of the False Teachers (6:2*b*-5)

"These duties" is more literally translated "these things." They are the teachings enunciated throughout the letter. The false teacher was anyone who taught "otherwise"—that is, whose teachings contradicted those of the apostle. A more serious charge is made. The false teacher "does not agree with the sound words of our Lord Jesus Christ." This is a rare reference in the epistles to the actual teachings of Jesus, although none are quoted in this letter. Behind the generally accepted teachings of the church must have lain the teachings of Jesus himself.

A negative description of the motivation of the false teacher is given. He is conceited, an "ignoramus" (NEB), with "a morbid craving for controversy." The "teaching which accords with godliness" (v. 3) results in a quiet, orderly Christian piety. The false teaching, which deals in speculations rather than a concern for godly living, produces hostility and dissension. It is disruptive. On the other hand, the central message of the Christian gospel reconciles and unites believers, producing a community of love.

Men who were caught up in the wrangling over speculations were characterized as "depraved in mind" (v. 5). Moral character rather than intellectual ability is the issue here. The problem is sin. The depraved mind is explained by the phrase "bereft of the truth." The mind not guided by the truth rooted in the Christ event (3:16) can only be depraved. It has no sure guide for understanding genuine Christian living.

The last criticism is a devastating one. The false teacher is accused of being motivated by a desire for "gain." He wants to make a profit from religion. We see that very early, the Christian religion was seized upon by people for personal exploitation. Religion is a fertile field for gain. If a person can convince others that he alone has power and truth and that through him alone people can get in touch with God, he is in a position to charge them for the privilege of sharing his power.

Religion and Money (6:6-10)

The accusation about the profiteering motive of false teachers led to statements about the relation between the believer and money. There is true "gain" in genuine Christian faith, but not in terms of enrichment in this world. Indeed, the Christian attitude toward things is to be the exact opposite of the greedy spirit. It is "contentment," being satisfied with what one has.

Material wealth has only a very limited and transient value. It operates only in the narrow space between birth and death. What good does it do to accumulate a storehouse of treasure only to die and leave it all? The only concern about material things in the physical life between birth and death should be limited to the basic necessities. No matter how much money we have, we can wear only one suit at a time or eat one meal at a time. In terms of his physical welfare, the person who has enough to eat and wear is as well off as the millionaire.

The opposite of contentment is a driving insecurity which creates the "desire to be rich." This desire can cause one to fall into "temptation." The temptation is to use immoral means to achieve the goal, to defraud one's neighbor, and to be stingy and insensitive to the needs of other less fortunate human beings.

The greedy person becomes entrapped by the "snare" of his own desires. In his anxiety and insecurity he sells his own soul and becomes the helpless victim of his drive for wealth. The end of such an individual is "ruin and destruction." Perhaps the writer was thinking about the eternal destiny of the individual who is rich in things but poverty-stricken in spiritual matters.

The RSV translation of verse 10 needs to be amended somewhat. The Greek text does not say that "the love of money is the root of all evils." Literally it says that it is *a* root of evil. It is *one* of the sources of evil. "All evils" probably should be translated "all kinds of evil" (TEV). Money is neither moral nor immoral. The problem lies in the attitude toward it—in the "love" for money. This is what causes people to steal, pillage, rob, defraud, drive hard, merciless bargains, and do "all kinds" of evil things. The Bible teaches us to love God, to love man, and to use things as responsible stewards of his creation. We turn God's order upside down when we love things and use God and people.

Jesus emphasized in his teaching that the great danger in money is that it can be a rival to God for man's affection and allegiance (Matt. 6:19-24). That idea is also implicit in our passage. "Craving" for wealth causes people to wander "away from the faith." That is, they become idolators. Their confidence and hope no longer rest in God. They turn from God to seek security and satisfaction in things.

"Pierced their hearts with many pangs" probably refers to the pangs of the guilty conscience suffered by people who become disloyal to God in their quest for wealth.

Charge to Timothy (6:11-16)

The false teachers were headed in one direction. The "man of God" was to pursue a course in exactly the opposite direction. He was to "shun" (literally, "flee from") the evil practices and goals denounced in the foregoing passage. He was to pursue "righteousness, godliness, faith," and so forth. These virtues stood at the opposite pole from the arrogance and materialism of the false teachers.

The Christian life of holiness always involves a negative and positive effort. Some things are to be avoided; some are to be embraced. The positive is always more important, however, for being Christian is far more than avoiding evil attitudes and practices.

Paul was fond of metaphors of the kind found in verse 12 taken from the Greek athletic contests. Christian living called for an effort similar to the effort and dedication of the athlete. "Fight the good fight" may also be translated "run the good race" (see NEB; TEV). The latter is probably better in view of the context. Running a race is compatible with the verb *pursue*. It is also in keeping with the following exhortation. At the end of the race the runner received the laurel wreath of the victor. The prize before the Christian runner was "eternal life."

Timothy had been "called" to receive eternal life. "Called" refers to the gracious initiative of God who issues the invitation which we accept when we believe. "Confession" probably refers to the baptismal confession made orally by new converts "in the presence of many witnesses"—that is, other believers. So the Christian life is a race. The beginning point is the believer's response to God's call. At the finish line he receives the prize, eternal life. In the meantime he is to run an unswerving course to that goal.

The writer's charge to Timothy is presented in a very solemn fashion. It was given "in the presence of God." Furthermore, it was given in the presence of "Christ Jesus." He is the great example of the faithful witness who gives his "testimony" in the face of certain death. Christ's witness to God was made before the pagan judge Pontius Pilate. The implication is that followers of Christ are to give their Christian testimony no matter what the cost.

Timothy was charged to "keep the commandment," but we cannot know exactly what this means. In general, of course, this letter defines what the author considered to be the duty of Timothy. The soldier of Jesus Christ has the responsibility of faithful obedience until his "appearing."

In connection with the appearing of the Lord at the end of the age Paul emphasized two or three ideas. That appearing is certain. It will be brought about by a sovereign, transcendent God. It will take place "at the proper time." This phrase means the time that God has chosen.

Further Warning Against Materialism (6:17-19)

From the available evidence we conclude that the churches did not have many rich members. As time went on, however, their number probably grew as the churches grew. This passage shows that some, at least, had to deal with the temptation presented by wealth.

One problem of the riches was the threat to Christian fellowship. A rich person might be tempted "to be haughty" in relationship to the poor. Another problem is the one we have mentioned. He could find his security in his wealth rather than in God. The author underlined the folly of this by the use of the adjective "uncertain" to modify "riches." God is the source of the gifts which make for genuine happiness.

The possession of wealth is not seen as an evil in itself. It was dangerous, but it also offered an opportunity for the expression of genuine Christian character. Money is to be used "to do good." The truly "rich" is the person who uses his money for "good deeds." The spirit of the giver is to match his actions. He is to be "liberal and generous."

Money, then, can be used as a way of making a genuine investment in the future. The only money which has a relationship to the future of the believers is that which serves the purpose of Christian compassion. Generous persons are "laying up for themselves a good foundation for the future." Having spurned the false security of money and having trusted in God, there is real underpinning to their confidence about the future. In essence they are taking "hold of the life which is life indeed." Their generous use of money, therefore, is interpreted as a concrete expression of his faith in the security God provides.

Final Warning to Timothy (6:20-21)

This final exhortation to Timothy once again involves both the positive and negative aspects of Christian living. He is to "guard" the genuine teachings of the gospel. They have been given to him as a trust. In each generation much depends on the faithfulness of ministers to that trust.

He is to avoid the kinds of ideas which have threatened the sound teachings of the faith. The false teachers thought they were superior and wise and that their words were very significant. Paul spoke of their talk in a very depreciating way. It was "godless chatter." The false teachers claimed to reveal a superior "knowledge." Paul countered with the accusation that their message was full of contradictions.

The danger is clearly stated. A person who accepted the false claims of this seductive message would miss "the mark as regards the faith." Most of the modern versions agree with the idea expressed in the TEV: "they have lost the way of faith." This is the only way that leads to the goal of eternal life.

In this tension in which he found himself, Timothy needed "grace" above all. He needed the presence, help, and love of a gracious God. That is exactly what Paul wished for him in the closing words of the letter.

2 TIMOTHY

Introduction

From 2 Timothy we learn that Paul was in prison when he wrote this letter (1:8; 2:9). The outlook was bleak, and the apostle apparently believed that he would be executed (4:6).

Prior to this time he had visited Troas (4:13), Corinth, and Miletus (4:20). But these movements of the apostle Paul do not fit into what Acts and the letters tell us of his life. According to a favorite hypothesis (see Introduction to 1 Tim.), 2 Timothy was written in Rome during Paul's second imprisonment, just prior to his death.

The instructions given to Timothy in the letter presuppose the same kind of heresy described in the first epistle to him. Paul called upon his associate to resist harmful, false teachings and to remain true to that which he had learned from the apostle himself.

Charge to Timothy

1:1 to 2:7

The Salutation (1:1-2)

Often in his salutation Paul referred to his apostleship. "Apostle" means "one who is sent" and could be used to designate an emissary sent out by a church.

"According to the promise of the life" is a literal translation of the Greek text. It is possible to interpret the phrase to mean "sent to proclaim the promised life" (TEV). The emphasis in this greeting is on the life that God has promised. Paul probably wrote this at the very end of his life. He was well aware of his impending death (see 4:6-8). The promise of life was more precious to Paul than it had ever been before.

The letter is addressed to Timothy, an associate of Paul since the second missionary journey (Acts 16:3). The phrase "my beloved child" underscores the special relationship between the older apostle and the younger helper. Paul may have won Timothy to Christ. We know that he regarded the young man as his son in the ministry. There was a great bond of love between the two. (For comments on the greeting see 1 Tim. 1:2.)

Thanksgiving and Longing (1:3-4)

Paul's letters ordinarily include a thanksgiving at the beginning. Exceptions are Galatians, 1 Timothy, and Titus. His gratitude to God for Timothy was a consistent element in his prayers for his younger associate. The apostle claimed to serve the God to whom he prayed "with a clear conscience." This probably means that in his apostolic ministry as a Christian Jew, he was convinced that he was truly serving the God who is revealed in the Old Testament.

Paul served the God whom his "fathers" served. For Paul the Christian gospel was the fulfillment of the message of the Old Testament. The Christian church was a continuation of God's purpose to create Israel, the redeemed community. Both he and his ancestors were loyal to the same God and were involved in the same redemptive purpose. He was no traitor to his past.

The last parting between Paul and Timothy had been painful and emotional. Paul vividly remembered Timothy's tears. He experienced constant longing to be reunited with his friend. The parting and the memory of it were painful; the reunion would bring joy.

Reminders of the Past (1:5-7)

Paul was well aware of the difficulties and dangers confronted by Timothy in his ministry. He was deeply concerned that the younger man discharge his responsibility faithfully and well. He knew that Timothy had had a good beginning and reminded him of that.

In his "sincere faith" Timothy possessed that without which a valid ministry was impossible. The word "sincere" is used to modify faith because there were numbers of people who claimed to believe but who gave no evidence that their faith was genuine. Paul wrote a great deal about these false believers in the Pastorals.

Timothy's faith was of the same character as that of his "grandmother" and "mother." We know nothing more of "Lois" than is mentioned here. From Acts 16:1 we learn that "Eunice" was a Jewish

Christian, and her husband was a Greek, presumably an unbeliever.

Paul also believed that Timothy had received a "gift" for ministry. There are several ideas which emerge from Paul's statement. When God calls a person to ministry, he equips him to fulfill that calling. Whatever Timothy had to offer in the service of God was not to be thought of as his own ability or his own achievement. It was a "gift of God."

To be a recipient of a gift implies responsibility. So Paul urged Timothy to "stir into flame the gift of God" (NEB) which was in him. The gift can lie dormant unless it is cultivated and used by the recipient.

In Timothy's case Paul feared that the hostile environment and opposition to his ministry might make Timothy hesitant to exercise his gift. "Timidity" or cowardice is not an expression of God's Spirit. Neither are weakness, hatred, and loose and immoral living. God's Spirit manifests itself in "power and love and self-control."

Timothy's gift came to him, said Paul, "through the laying on of my hands." The reference is, of course, to ordination. In 1 Timothy 4:14 the writer says that the council of elders laid hands on Timothy. Paul's statement in 2 Timothy does not rule out the possibility that others joined in the ordination of Timothy. "Through the laying on of my hands" does not mean that ordination confers the gifts for ministry any more than baptism confers salvation. Ordination is a channel through which God works. It is God who gives the gifts.

A Partner in Suffering for the Gospel (1:8-10)

Now we come to the point of Paul's major concern. He was aware that Timothy was being tested by opposition to the genuine gospel of Jesus Christ. The opposition no doubt came from without and within the churches. Paul's primary emphasis in the Pastorals, however, is on the problems within the churches themselves.

Because of the pressures Timothy could lose his courage, become "ashamed," and fail to bear his witness to the Lord. Here we perceive Paul's conception of genuine preaching. The preacher's task is to testify to his Lord.

Paul knew what it was to be deserted by his associates. Many people did not want to be identified with a man who was an accused prisoner of the state. He asked Timothy not to join that number. When hardships come, the genuine minister recognizes that he is not to isolate himself from the gospel or from those who suffer for it. Rather, he

is to "share" with them in their trials. The minister is not left to his
own resources as he suffers for the gospel. He is supported and
strengthened by "the power of God," the strength which comes from
God, given to his faithful witness.

The persecuted servant of God is also to be aware of what God
has done for his people."[He] saved us." Usually Paul was referring
to the ultimate triumph of God's people when he spoke of their salvation. Here he referred to what God had already done. We generally
speak of being saved when we refer to conversion. God "called us
with a holy calling." The word "holy" refers first of all to God and
then describes anything or anybody who belongs to him. The holy
calling is that calling by which God constitutes his community. The
TEV, for example, translates the phrase "called us to be his own people." Saving us and making us his people are not two different things;
they are one and the same. The ultimate purpose of saving individuals
is to incorporate them into the redeemed community. None of this
is our achievement. It is all due to God's gracious redemptive "purpose." The false teaching disturbing the churches seems to have emphasized the keeping of the law. This was a perversion of the gospel.
Our salvation is possible only through God's grace. In order to make
this point clear, the author made a very interesting statement. He
said that God gave his grace to us "ages ago." How can we take
credit for something that was already in existence before we were
born?

In due time this grace "was manifested," revealed in a concrete
historical way, in the death of "our Savior Christ Jesus." The ultimate
reaches of salvation were determined in that event. Jesus "abolished"
or brought an end to the power of death. In his resurrection he showed
the limits of death's power and established the victory of life over
death. The statements in verses 9 and 10 constitute one of the summa-
ries of the gospel which we find here and there in Paul's letters.

The Example of Paul's Commitment (1:11-14)

"This gospel" of salvation and eternal life through God's grace manifested in Christ is the one in whose service God had placed Paul.
The apostle used three words to describe his ministry. He was
"preacher and apostle and teacher." The word for preacher means
"herald." It emphasized Paul's responsibility, which he shared with
all preachers, to proclaim the good news of God's saving deed. As
an apostle he was Christ's special representative with particular re-

sponsibility for the mission to the Gentiles. The task of teaching was his because he was responsible for leading converts to grow in their new life.

Paul was a prisoner facing death because of his commitment to the gospel. But he was not "ashamed." The verb "to be ashamed" means basically to lose confidence. Paul's confidence was unflagging because of his personal acquaintance with the Lord in whom he had placed his trust. As he put it, "I know who it is in whom I have trusted" (NEB).

His confidence was based on the conviction that Jesus Christ guaranteed the continuation and victory of the gospel. "What has been entrusted to me" is the RSV translation of an ambiguous phrase. It can also mean "What I have [entrusted] to him" (as in the KJV). The same key word is found in verse 14. There it surely must be understood as that which had been entrusted to Timothy.

Both translations make sense in verse 12. But our translators were probably right in taking it as a reference to what God had entrusted to Paul. Probably we should understand this as the truth of the gospel. Paul was in prison. He probably would be executed. But this would not stop the gospel. Its future was guaranteed by the power of his Lord and was not related to the fate of its herald.

Paul asked Timothy to be true to the same message. He was to "follow the pattern" of the apostle, with the courage that comes from "faith" and the spirit of "love," not of hostility and hatred.

A Personal Note (1:15-18)

A poignant, personal note intrudes at this point. The apostle in prison was saddened because he had been deserted by people who should have supported him. We do not know at what point the people in Asia had turned away from him. Asia was the Roman province whose chief city was Ephesus. There is nothing in Acts or Paul's other letters to help us here. We do not know the cause of the desertion. Two people are mentioned, perhaps because their failure was especially painful to Paul. Of the two men, Phygelus and Hermogenes, we know nothing beyond what Paul wrote here.

In the midst of the painful memories there was one who brought comfort to Paul. Onesiphorus had been a source of spiritual refreshment for him. He had traveled to Rome while Paul was a prisoner there. Instead of avoiding the accused man, Onesiphorus had searched for him "eagerly." His conduct at that time was an expression of his willingness to serve, so well demonstrated in Ephesus.

Paul prayed that Onesiphorus would "find mercy from the Lord on that day" (the day of judgment). This underlines the fact that even a person like Onesiphorus cannot depend upon his own works for salvation. He, like all others, must depend solely on the mercy of God in the future judgment.

The Good Soldier (2:1-7)

Two aspects of the ministry are emphasized in the first two verses. First, there is the necessity to withstand the hostile attacks to which God's servant is subjected. For this he needs strength. The source of strength is God's "grace" which belongs to us "in [our union with] Christ Jesus." Second, there is the active aspect of ministry. Timothy's main responsibility was defined by the circumstances of the day. There were people who were perverting the gospel. It was Timothy's responsibility to do what he could to see that the genuine gospel was preserved for others.

The truth was what Timothy had learned from Paul. He had heard it "before many witnesses." Perhaps this remark was made because of certain teachings by people we call Gnostics. They claimed that the truth was a mystery that could only be revealed in secret to those who sought initiation. Paul declared that his gospel was an open and public matter.

This truth, which Paul defined in 1:9-10 and which we encounter again in 2:8-13, was to be transmitted to "faithful men." This means reliable or trustworthy men. In addition to this attribute, they also should possess competence as teachers. Their purpose was to serve as links in the chain of gospel witness.

Paul returned to the theme of the necessity to suffer for the gospel. He used several metaphors to develop the theme. The first is that of the "soldier." The Christian is unlike the soldier in one major respect. He does not inflict harm on others. There are two aspects of the soldier's life, however, that parallel the Christian's life. For one thing, the good soldier is able to stand against the assault of the enemy. For another, his devotion to his commander is complete. He does not become "entangled in civilian pursuits." His commitment has a motive. His only desire is "to satisfy the one" under whose command he enlisted.

Perhaps Paul was saying to Timothy that he should devote himself fully to the gospel. The concept of a full-time ministry is firmly entrenched in Christian circles today. The idea behind it is that some ministers need to give themselves wholly to their ministry and not become involved with other matters.

Paul uses two metaphors in his portrayal of the ministry, the "athlete" and the "farmer." The main idea in both seems to be that their devotion and discipline were due to their expectation of the future. The Olympic athlete had to train and compete by the rules or he would be disqualified from the competition. The farmer had to work hard if he expected to enjoy the fruits of the harvest.

The Christian life involves sacrifice, discipline, and hard work. But the hoped-for prize makes it all worthwhile. The athlete expected to receive a crown of laurel wreath if he won. The believer expects to receive the crown of eternal life. These were some of the lessons Paul hoped Timothy would understand when he wrote: "Think over what I say."

The Gospel and Its Enemies

2:8-26

The Heart of the Gospel (2:8-10)

The good minister of the gospel must keep his attention centered on Jesus Christ. Failure in ministry can often be attributed to distractions that cause us to focus on some other person or thing. Two very important truths about Jesus Christ were mentioned by Paul. They are his resurrection and his incarnation. Paul was saying in essence that the Jesus who was raised was the one who fulfilled Jewish messianic expectations as a descendant of David. In contrast to the false teachers opposed in the Pastorals, Paul's preaching was about Jesus Christ, the risen Messiah.

Because of his faithfulness in proclaiming the good news ("gospel") of God's salvation in Jesus Christ alone, Paul had been arrested and was "wearing fetters" at the time this epistle was written. He had to bear the abuse and shame accorded a common criminal. Indeed, he was so regarded by the legal authorities. But one fact cheered the apostle even at this, the lowest moment of his life. Man may chain the preacher, but they cannot chain the "word of God." In all the places where Paul had preached, the word of God was a free, powerful, transforming force.

All of Paul's suffering was made infinitely worthwhile because of the importance of the ministry for which he was paying such a fearful price. Paul had to be faithful to the gospel, whatever the cost, for the "sake of the elect." The "elect" is one of the terms for the people of God in the Bible. It emphasizes the fact that they belong to God because God chose them and not because they chose him.

Election is completed in "glory." Paul knew that his faithfulness to the gospel played a part in God's grand purpose for his people. "Salvation" is used in verse 10 in the way that Paul generally used it outside the Pastorals. It does not refer to conversion but to the eventual deliverance and triumph of God's people over the power of sin and death.

A Trustworthy Saying (2:11-13)

"The saying is sure" indicates that the statement which follows was one commonly heard in Christian circles, perhaps in the worship of the churches. It inspired believers who were suffering for their faith and who even faced the grim prospect of death. The suffering of this present time is made worthwhile because of the Christian hope. Death can be faced because it is followed by resurrection. Persecution at the hands of earthly authorities can be endured because of the expectation of sharing in Christ's reign.

On the other hand, if people deny the Lord under the pressure of persecution, they cannot expect to be confessed by him before the heavenly Judge. The churches in early centuries faced the problem on many occasions of what to do with people who had denied Christ under persecution. Some people favored accepting them back into the church. Others took the position that such persons had forfeited their hope of eternal life. The latter made use of just such texts as this to prove their point.

Paul underlined the fact that denial of our faith is a very serious matter. His purpose was to keep people from denying their Lord when confronted by hostility. Persons who fail to confess Jesus as Savior and Lord, whatever the circumstances, have committed a grave sin. They need to be aware of that.

This strong and severe affirmation is a part of the demand of the gospel. But what is the word of the gospel to those who fail? It is not the word of demand but the word of grace. "If we confess our sins, he is faithful and just, and will forgive our sins" (1 John 1:9). The gospel consists both of demand and grace. The demand is to help us to be faithful. "Grace" is the word that comes to us in our unfaithfulness.

Verse 13 is probably Paul's addition to the "sure saying." In the saying certain parallels are drawn between the believer's actions and Christ's. But the writer wanted to make it crystal clear that there was one area where no parallel existed. Human beings are very often unfaithful. This is not true of Christ. He is never unfaithful. We can always trust him to act according to his character and promises.

Christ cannot be unfaithful because "he cannot deny himself." Such action would be a contradiction of his being. Our problem arises because of the contradictions which exist within us. We are Christians, and we sometimes act in accordance with our new nature. But we are also in the world. We are still subject to the power of evil. We have been redeemed, but our redemption is not yet complete. We sometimes act, therefore, contrary to our nature as God's redeemed people. There is no such division in the person of Christ. His nature is not subject to the tensions and contradictions which characterize ours. He is consistently faithful to himself.

Handling the Word of Truth (2:14-19)

In this passage Paul began to make explicit remarks about the false approach to the gospel which he expected Timothy to resist. It is only now, therefore, that we begin to get some idea about the nature of the heresy which threatened the churches.

Faithfulness to Christ and his gospel, as Paul had outlined it, was the watchword. Witness to the gospel (1:8) is set over against becoming involved in "disputing about words." The constant shame of the church from those early days has been the disputes among believers over ideas and words. The unifying center of the church is an event—what God did in Jesus Christ. The unifying task of the church is her mission—the proclamation of that event.

For Paul one test of truth was its result in the lives of people. The proclamation of the gospel brings salvation and transformed lives. Arguing about words "only ruins the hearers." Paul was talking about spiritual ruin. The squabbling over speculative ideas did not lead people to know God. It led in the other direction.

"Do your best" pleases God. "As one approved" (v. 15) translates an adjective which describes a person who has demonstrated his character in the midst of the trials to which he has been subjected. It could be used of the soldier who had proved his courage and loyalty in the heat of battle. The believer faces many kinds of tests and temptations in his life. The question is whether he has so conducted himself as to merit God's approbation and not man's. If we can do this, we have no cause to be "ashamed" of our work. The unashamed "workman" is the one who can face his employer with confidence in a job well done.

The basic idea in "rightly handling" is clear from the context. Timothy is not to follow the course of the false teachers. They are engaged in pernicious theological "chatter" which destroys the hearer. Timothy is to take the opposite approach. As we can see from the versions, the exact nuance of the participle translated "rightly handling" is not altogether clear. We find various translations: "Be straightforward in your proclamation of the truth" (NEB); "one who correctly teaches the message of God's truth" (TEV).

We know what Paul considered to be the "word," or message, "of truth." He expressed it in 2:8. We also know that Paul believed the preacher's task was to proclaim this message and not become involved in speculative religious notions. The false teachers claimed to be teaching about God, but Paul called what they were doing "godless chatter." It led people further and further away from God. It was a pernicious evil that could not be contained. It was a poison, spreading like "gangrene." This is a strong metaphor, underlining the genuine fears of the writer.

In verse 18 we come across one of the doctrines being spread by the destructive persons in the church. Only two of the false teachers, Hymenaeus and Philetus, are mentioned by name. They taught that the resurrection of believers had already taken place.

We can only guess at the content of their teaching. They were probably more Greek than Jewish in their view of life beyond death. Like the Gnostics of the second century, they probably thought that the body was basically inferior or perhaps evil. Only the soul or spirit was immortal and eternal.

They probably had latched on to a metaphor used by Paul himself. He talked of conversion as being raised with Christ (Col. 3:1). But he also believed in the redemption of the body. Bodily existence was essential to true existence. According to Paul, believers would be clothed with a body appropriate to their existence in glory through the resurrection of the body from the dead.

We can assume, therefore, that the false teachers denied the possibility of any future resurrection. They held that the resurrection of believers had taken place at conversion. They had moved into the sphere of immortal life at that time. Upon death the spirit, thus transformed, would discard the body and never be associated with a body again.

For Paul the resurrection of believers was a vital part of the Christian proclamation. Belief in it was essential to the faith of God's people. By teaching a doctrine of immortality rather than the resurrection, the false teachers were "upsetting the faith of some." Some people were so confused that they were forsaking some of the vital elements of their faith.

There are many ideas which are peripheral to the gospel. We need to be able to understand this so that we do not make something central when it is not. But at the very core of the gospel stands the death and resurrection of Jesus Christ and what this means in the lives of believers. When people start changing this, they are tampering with that which is most vital.

Paul was disturbed and concerned because of what was happening in the churches. But he was not pessimistic. His confidence was not placed in men; it was placed in God. The future of the gospel cause did not depend on what men knew about God but upon God's knowledge of man.

The false teachers could fool and confuse other people. They might even be popular and powerful. But this did not guarantee their success and future. The foundation of the work of redemption rests on this truth: "The Lord knows those who are his." The genuine believer can take comfort and hope from this confidence. Men may reject him, but God knows him. On the other hand, the false members should be aware also of this fact. They may fool man, but they cannot fool God.

The quotation in verse 19 comes from Numbers 16:5. Timothy and other Christians would be reminded immediately about the circumstances in which the words were spoken. Korah, Dathan, and Abiram had led a rebellion against Moses. The earth had opened up and swallowed the rebellious men and their families. God knew who were not his, and his judgment fell upon them.

Faithful servants of God have a responsibility in such situations. Paul wrote: "Let every one who names the name of the Lord depart from iniquity." In the story in Numbers 16, people faithful to Moses were advised to separate themselves from the wicked men, lest they also suffer the judgment about to fall on them. The meaning is clear in 2 Timothy. Faithful Christians are to separate themselves from the false teachers who stand under God's judgment.

Vessels, Good and Bad (2:20-26)

Paul used an interesting illustration to describe the condition of the church. He compared it to "a great house," a house owned by a wealthy person. The rich person, who lived in a large house, possessed "vessels of gold and silver." These were reserved for special occasions. They were not put to common, ordinary use. For the daily needs of the household there were cheaper, commonplace vessels of "wood and earthenware." One did not use the gold and silver utensils to serve slaves of the household, for example. The best utensils were used at dinner for honored guests.

The church consisted of members who could be compared to the vessels in the affluent home. There were "noble and ignoble" vessels in the church. The difference, to be sure, was not based upon intrinsic worth. No Christian is inferior to any other Christian. Paul made it clear that the classification of believers was determined by their own personal moral discipline.

The believer who "purifies himself" is a noble vessel. There is a paradox in the Christian life. On the one hand, all our strength comes from God. On the other, we are all responsible for the level of our commitment to God. We are responsible for being honorable, pure, and committed to the genuine gospel of Jesus Christ. Never does the emphasis on our total dependence on God take away our moral responsibility to live a disciplined Christian life.

Paul seemed to imply that all believers have some use. We may limit our usefulness, however, by the level of our consecration. The believer who purifies himself will not limit his use by the Master of God's household in any way. In the words of our translation, he will be "ready for any good work."

In this disciplined Christian life there is both a negative and a positive aspect. Paul stressed the negative first: "Shun youthful passions." The word translated "shun" means literally "flee." The word translated "passions" means desires, whether good or evil. In the New Testament, however, it is most often used of evil or wayward impulses. It was axiomatic in Paul's day, as well as ours, that young people had greater difficulty than their elders in dealing with the "wayward impulses of youth" (NEB). These were desires that conflicted with the purpose of God for the life. Paul's advice to Timothy was urgent. Do not nurture and play with these desires. Run from them as fast as you can.

The positive goals of the believer's life are "righteousness, faith, love, and peace." Some of these words may be given more than one meaning. Thus, righteousness may also be translated "justice," a fitting concern of the Christian. Or the emphasis may be upon one's own personal character. Faith can be our trust in God, or it can also refer to our own trustworthiness, integrity, or faithfulness (NEB).

The pursuit of the goals of Christian character and conduct is not an individual matter. It takes place in the context of the church, in fellowship "with all those who call upon the name of the Lord." "From a pure heart" may also be translated "in singleness of mind" (NEB). The heart is the center of man as an intelligent, willing being. The contrast is with the false teachers who serve the Lord with mixed impure motives.

One of the main interests of the writer of the Pastorals was the unity of the church. "Stupid, senseless controversies" bred factions. The "Lord's servant" is not quarrelsome but is kind and gentle. He is an "apt," or good, "teacher," patient with those who resent and resist his ministry. Correction is not harsh but gentle. The good minister always has the hope that those who refuse the truth may "repent," turn around in their attitude and receive the "truth."

They are to be treated with compassion because they are the devil's victims. He has caught them in his "snare." They have become his prey, much as animals are captured in a trap. Consequently they are doing his "will" as they engage in their senseless controversies. But the power of God is greater than the power of the devil. There is always the possibility of "escape." The word for escape in Greek is interesting. It means "to become sober again," "to come to one's senses" (NEB). If they do come to their senses, those misguided people will "come to know the truth." The truth is not religious speculation or splitting hairs over dogma. It is the revelation of God's redemptive, loving purpose in Jesus Christ.

Warning About Impending Dangers
3:1 to 4:5

The Worsening Spiritual Climate (3:1-5)

It was axiomatic in apocalyptic literature that things were going to get worse before the end. The "last days" was a common expression used in Christian circles to refer to the period just prior to the return of Christ. The idea is that rebellion against God will reach new heights in its frenzy. All restraint will be loosed. The phrase is not used in the earlier Pauline epistles.

It seems that most early Christians looked for the return of the Lord soon. They felt that they were living in the "last days." Probably we should understand all the period beginning with the resurrection of Jesus as the last days. They are last days because there has been the constant possibility of the return of the Lord. We need to be wary, however, about predicting the time of the exact end of the world, remembering always the statement of Jesus:"But of that day and hour no one knows" (Mark 13:32).

Paul was primarily seeking to prevent Timothy from falling into discouragement and despair. "Times of stress" should not invoke a sense of defeat but rather of hope. They do not signal the victory of evil but its defeat.

The list of evils (v. 2) is not to be understood necessarily as precise descriptions of the false teachers. They constitute a general description and correspond to similar lists of vices that can be found elsewhere. Throughout history at certain times and in certain places, when social structures have broken down, these evils have been rampant. Unbridled egotism, greed, disregard for authority, and cruel, callous attitudes toward others are the kinds of things described here.

Paul applied the catalog of vices to the false religious teachers. They had a form of "religion." Their practices, vocabulary, and stated goals were similar and no doubt in some cases identical with those found in genuine religious teachers. But they were guilty of "denying the power" of true godliness. Their religion was sterile and weak, incapable of turning men to God and transforming lives. They were wolves in sheep's clothing.

Religious Charlatans (3:6-9)

Evidently the religion of the false teachers had a special appeal to certain women. The teachers under the guise of being true preachers of the gospel wormed their way into families. Certain kinds of people were especially susceptible. Paul characterized them as "weak . . . , burdened with sins," and vacillating because they were ruled by their conflicting "impulses." They were always ready to listen to any new teaching, thinking perhaps that it would bring them the release and contentment which they desired. But they never came to "a knowledge of the truth." The truth for Paul is the gospel of God's salvation in Jesus Christ. The speculations and theories of the false teachers led people away from Christ.

Paul's description could well have been written in the twentieth century. The air is filled with teachings of the cults. The adherents of many diverse groups, claiming to have an ultimate revelation of the truth, prey upon weak people who are longing for an answer to their problems of guilt, alienation, and a lack of self-worth.

Jannes and Jambres are not named in the Old Testament. They are mentioned in later literature as the magicians in Pharaoh's court who opposed Moses. They attempted to thwart him by performing miracles similar to those done by Moses. The false teachers could not have been denounced in stronger terms. They were not God's representatives; they were his enemies.

Their minds were "corrupt," the very opposite of the transformed mind. This meant that all the teaching devised by them was also corrupt. They failed all the tests of genuine faith (see NEB).

Paul was convinced that the success of such teachers was limited and temporary. Just as the impotence of the magicians opposed to Moses became apparent, so would the "folly" of the men who opposed the truth. Paul believed that truth would prevail and falsehood would be exposed eventually. God guaranteed the future of his redemptive purpose and work.

The Lot of the Faithful Minister (3:10-17)

The apostle's counsel to Timothy did not come from an "ivory tower" existence. He knew what it was to suffer hardship for the

gospel. From intimate association Timothy knew what kind of man
Paul was. He had observed or, literally, "followed" (NEB) the life of
Paul.

As a pupil who had learned from his master, Timothy knew what
Paul had taught. He was aware that his teaching had been consistent
in good times and bad. He also verified that Paul's "conduct" had
been consistent with his teaching. This is one of the real tests of the
genuine Christian teacher. Does he himself live by what he says?

Paul's "aim in life" was to serve his Lord. He had steadfastly pursued
this aim. He had not faltered in his faith, as could be attested in his
faithfulness. He had been patient with people who had misunderstood
and opposed him, responding to them in the spirit of "love." Timothy
had observed firsthand Paul's "steadfastness" under the stress of persecution. "Patience" describes the Christian attitude toward persons.
"Steadfastness" describes his attitude toward trying circumstances,
such as "persecutions" with their attendant "sufferings." The steadfast
person rejoices in the ultimate victory assured by God in the midst
of what seems to be defeat.

Paul had been thrown out of Antioch, had escaped a conspiracy
in Iconium, and had been stoned in Lystra. But in all of those experiences he had felt the presence and power of God, who was greater
than his enemies.

It was axiomatic for Paul that every genuine Christian would be
"persecuted." This was indeed the lot of believers in those days when
they constituted a despised and tiny minority in the midst of a hostile
world.

The enemies of the faith may seem to be victorious for the moment.
They are popular and prosperous. But Paul believed that evil "imposters" would go "from bad to worse." They could not gain the ultimate
victory because they were opposed to God. The "imposters" refers
to the false teachers, the "wolves in sheep's clothing."

Timothy was not without guidance as he faced the challenge of
the imposters. That guidance consisted of three elements. First, he
had learned the truth of the gospel from Paul's teaching and example.
Second, he had made a commitment of faith to Jesus Christ as
preached by Paul. Timothy was not to be severed from his original
commitment by new and attractive but deceptive teachings. Third,
Timothy had the help of "sacred writings." We may assume that these
were the Old Testament Scriptures. The point in Paul's admonition
was that Timothy was to be guided by written Scripture in addition

to the gospel. He was not to be influenced by the speculations and traditions of the false teachers.

Verse 16 cannot be translated with dogmatic assurance. The Greek grammar allows for two possibilities: (1) "All scripture is inspired" (as in the RSV); and (2) "Every scripture inspired by God is also" (see RSV footnote). No doubt there were writings which Paul would not have regarded as inspired. That, however, is hardly Paul's point. Nor can we deduce from this and other references an exact doctrine of inspiration. Paul believed that God inspired men to write scriptures. He also believed that the Christian found these profitable in a number of ways. They could be used to teach the truth, always in the light of God's supreme revelation in Jesus Christ. They could be used "for reproof" (to rebuke error) and for "correction" (to help people to bring their lives under God's judgment). They could also be used in the positive sense of "training in righteousness." That is, they could guide people in right living.

When "the man of God," the teacher, uses Scripture in this way, he will be "complete," lacking nothing for his ministry. He will be "equipped for every good work." That is, he will be prepared for any kind of ministry for which God wishes to use him. He will not have the kinds of limitations that might make him useless for certain tasks.

Faithfulness to the Word (4:1-5)

Paul's final injunction to Timothy is couched in the most solemn and serious language. He delivered it conscious of the "presence of God and Christ Jesus." Both Paul and Timothy finally had to answer to God, not to man. The seriousness and solemnity of the charge were heightened by the convictions expressed in verse 1. Jesus Christ would return in glory. He would be the Judge of those who were still alive at his coming. Nor would the dead escape the judgment, for they would also appear before him. Finally Jesus Christ would reign as king of the universe. It is, therefore, a serious matter to receive a charge that had his authority.

Paul defined the task for which Timothy was responsible. He was to "preach the word." The word translated "preach" is one of several Greek verbs in the New Testament that can be so translated. This verb means to proclaim as a herald. The herald of the gospel is judged in terms of his faithfulness in proclaiming the message of Christ. We often identify "the word" with the Bible. It is not used in this way in the New Testament. The Word is God's Word. Specifically, it is the proclamation that he has acted to save men through Jesus Christ.

Paul defined the time when the message is to be preached. It is to be proclaimed on every occasion. "In season" means when it seems opportune to preach it. "Out of season" refers to those occasions when it does not seem appropriate to proclaim it. The preacher is to proclaim the message in every possible way. He is to "convince," use all the arguments in his arsenal. He is to "rebuke." The sad aspect of the preacher's task is his responsibility to call people under God's judgment because of their rebellion and sin. He is to "exhort" (appeal passionately to his hearers to turn to Jesus Christ).

The spirit of the preacher is extremely important. His preaching and teaching are to be characterized by "patience." He is not to allow the hostile reaction of his hearers to determine his attitude toward them or to deter him in his attempts to win them. Paul knew that patience would be extremely important in the course of Timothy's ministry. His teaching would be ignored, and people would reject him to flock to other teachers.

For Paul "sound teaching" was the message of the gospel that leads to unity and love. Many teachers of gospel truth have experienced exactly what Paul predicted would happen. People reject them as being old-fashioned and dull. Paul said the problem was "itching ears."

People often reject the truth of the gospel because they long for something sensational and new. They collect "teachers to suit their own likings." How many preachers have experienced rejection because they did not say what their listeners wanted to hear! Paul foresaw the tragic result. Such people would "turn away from listening to the truth and wander into myths." "Myths" was Paul's way of referring to the speculative ideas with which some people wanted to replace the gospel.

What is to be the stance of the preacher when he sees this situation develop? He is to remain "steady" or poised, suffer any hardship that results from his faithfulness, "do the work of an evangelist" (a preacher of the gospel), and "fulfill" his "ministry" by doing everything that he has been called to do to the very end of his life.

Paul's Valedictory

4:6-22

The Impending End (4:6-8)

In this passage Paul shared with us his own attitude and faith in the face of his impending execution. His statements could have been dictated just days or even hours before his death. We are enabled to see how one great Christian viewed the possibility of sacrificing his own life for the gospel. It is one of the noblest and most inspirational passages of the Bible.

Paul used a sacrificial image to portray his own death. The verb translated "am . . . being sacrificed" means "to pour out as a drink offering." Some other versions emphasize this meaning more clearly, as, for example, the NEB: "My life is being poured out on the altar."

From the point of view of the authorities, Paul was a criminal. When they executed him, they were giving him what he deserved. But Paul gave to his prospective death a much higher meaning. Just as the priests in Jerusalem poured the drink offering on the altar, so his own life's blood would be poured out as an offering to God (see Rev. 6:9 for a similar idea).

On other occasions Paul had been rescued from impending danger. At this writing, however, he had a sense that his life's work had been finished. Psychiatrists tell us that the people who lead the fullest lives seem to fear death least. Those whose lives have been empty of meaning and fulfillment are morbid and depressed by the thought of death. Paul certainly found life full of meaning and faced the end with confidence and hope. The "time," or appropriate moment, for Paul's departure had arrived.

There were no regrets. Paul had felt that he was nearing the goal toward which he had been striving. We may compare this idea with an earlier one found in Philippians 3:13-14. There Paul was still "straining forward" toward the goal. Here there is the sense of peace and satisfaction at being so near its realization.

The metaphors from athletics of which Paul was so fond once again become vehicles for expressing his thought. There is some doubt about whether a wrestling match, as in the RSV, or a race (NEB, TEV) was in Paul's mind in the first statement of verse 7. Perhaps it is the latter. If so, we hear Paul saying two things. He had run a good race, observing the rules and giving every ounce of energy and strength. Furthermore, he had run it to the finish line. So many people never finish the race.

Paul had been true to his commitment to Jesus Christ. He had encountered discouragement, obstacles, temptations, and competing ideas. He had passed the test and had proved himself loyal to his Lord under the most adverse of circumstances. Indeed, even at this late hour he could conceivably have averted his execution had he been willing to deny his Lord. But he could say with great satisfaction: "I have kept the faith."

When a runner in the athletic contest of the first century crossed the finish line as the victor in the race, he was assured of receiving the emblem of victory. It was a crown or wreath of laurel, pine, or olive leaves.

Paul was also sure that he would receive a victor's crown. But this is not a perishable crown that will wither and fade away. It is the "crown of righteousness." The phrase is ambiguous. Does it mean that righteousness is the crown which he will receive? Or does it mean that the crown is one that will be given to him because of the righteousness which was his through faith in Christ? In any case the crown is eternal life.

The person who is faithful to the Lord can confidently expect to receive his crown. The reason for his confidence is the character of the one who awards the victor's trophy. He is a "righteous judge." The time when the award will be made is called "that Day." It is the day of God's final victory over the forces of evil. It is the judgment day, when the sheep will be separated from the goats.

There is another important idea. In the races with which Paul was familiar and upon which he drew for his analogies, only one person won. In the Christian race, however, there is no limit to the number of victors. Included in the number are all "who have loved his appearing." "His appearing" refers to the great event of the future when the Lord will appear in glory.

Personal Notes (4:9-18)

Instructions to Timothy (4:9-15).—When he wrote these verses, Paul seemed to have been convinced of the nearness of his death. There must have been some possibility, however, that there would be further delay in the execution of the sentence imposed on him. He urged Timothy, therefore, to come to him soon.

The picture of Paul that emerges from his comments is a poignant one. He faces the end almost alone. Demas had deserted him. In Philemon 24 Paul included Demas in a list of "fellow workers." We long for details to help us understand what lies behind a tragic desertion. Paul told us only that Demas was "in love with this present world." This is the very opposite of those who love the Lord's appearing (4:8). Perhaps Demas did not want to risk being identified with a condemned man.

Others had gone elsewhere, presumably to discharge their responsibilities as Christian workers. Crescens had gone to Galatia. Titus, one of Paul's closest missionary associates, had gone to Dalmatia. Tychicus (Acts 20:4; Eph. 6:21; Col. 4:7; Titus 3:12) had been dispatched by Paul to Ephesus. Luke (Col. 4:14; Philemon 24) alone was left with Paul.

Paul wanted Timothy to bring Mark with him. Mark had provoked the anger of Paul when he deserted him during the first missionary journey (Acts 13:13). Subsequently, Paul refused to take him along on the next trip (Acts 15:37-38). It is good to know that the two were close friends again before Paul's death (see also Col. 4:10). Paul's former opinion of Mark had evidently changed drastically, for he described the younger man as "very useful in serving me."

Paul had left his cloak with Carpus in Troas. The cloak was a heavy woolen garment with a hole in it for the head to go through. It was useful in cold or rainy weather. Does this mean that Paul was suffering from the cold in his prison?

The apostle asked Timothy to bring the cloak along with the books and parchments. The books were papyrus rolls. The parchments were of vellum, specially prepared animal skins. There have been many guesses about the nature of these books and parchments. It may be, however, that nothing was written on them. Writing materials were precious, and perhaps Paul needed them for his own writing.

Paul singled out Alexander the coppersmith for special mention as an enemy of the gospel. An Alexander is mentioned in 1 Timothy 1:20 and another in Acts 19:33-34, but we cannot positively identify this man with either of those. The reason Paul mentioned him was that he was still active in his opposition to the gospel.

A personal testimony (4:16-18).—The "first defense" mentioned by Paul may have been a trial connected with a previous imprisonment. Whatever the case, Paul found himself completely deserted by men. No one came forward as a witness for the defense. No Christian in the vicinity wanted to be identified with the accused man.

But Paul had not been deserted completely. "The Lord [had] stood" by him when no one else dared to do so. From his Lord Paul had received the "strength" to carry on. Interestingly, Paul did not mention his defense. He was interested in proclaiming "the message fully" rather than in saving himself. Every circumstance of his life was seen by the apostle as an opportunity to preach the gospel.

Paul wrote that the Lord had rescued him "from the lion's mouth." This has been taken to imply that he was freed as a result of that trial. Paul's hope for the future was based upon his experience with God in the past. He believed that his Lord would rescue him "from every evil." He would save his servant "for his heavenly kingdom." This does not mean that Paul anticipated freedom from all earthly danger. We know that he expected to be executed. But the Lord would rescue him from the power of death.

Final Greetings (4:19-22)

As was customary in letter writing in the first century, Paul concluded his letter with personal greetings. Priscilla and Aquila had been friends and associates of Paul since his Corinthian ministry (Acts 18:2). Paul had praised Onesiphorus previously in this letter (1:16-18). In Romans 16:23 an Erastus is treasurer of the church in Corinth. Trophimus, an Ephesian, was a traveling companion of Paul on his last trip to Jerusalem (Acts 20:4; 21:29). The other people mentioned by Paul are unknown to us.

During winter, ships were unable to travel because of stormy weather. Paul, therefore, urged Timothy to "come before winter," so there would not be additional delay.

"Your" in verse 22 is singular and refers to Timothy. "You" is plural and includes the Christians with Timothy. This is not clear in the RSV, but note the NEB. The presence of the Lord and the outpouring of his grace was the greatest benefit that Paul could wish for Timothy and other believers.

TITUS

Introduction

Titus is one of the three Pastoral Epistles, so called because they give instructions about church order and Christian living. It is addressed to one of Paul's close missionary associates.

Titus

Most of the information we have about Titus is found in Galatians and 2 Corinthians. When Paul made his second trip to Jerusalem after his conversion, Titus, a Gentile, went with him (Gal. 2:1-10). He became the focus of controversy when some Jewish Christians attempted to force Paul to circumcise him. This Paul refused to do.

When Paul was still in Ephesus (Acts 19:1 to 20:1), he sent Titus as his emissary to deal with problems that had arisen in the hostile and rebellious church in Corinth. Subsequently, the apostle left Ephesus, hoping that Titus would meet him in Troas (2 Cor. 2:13). Disappointed and anxious when Titus did not arrive, Paul then journeyed to Macedonia. Titus came to him there and brought the joyous news that the Corinthian church was reconciled to her apostle (2 Cor. 7:6).

Paul sent Titus back to Corinth with the letter which we call 2 Corinthians (2 Cor. 8:6). His mission was to supervise the raising of the offering for the poor Christians in Jerusalem.

Occasion of the Letter

Paul had left Titus in Crete to organize the churches better and to instruct them so that they might resist dangerous false teachings (1:5). The heresy is of the same nature as that dealt with in 1 and 2 Timothy (see Introduction to 1 Tim.).

The same problem occurs here that we observed in the letters to Timothy. Neither Acts nor any other Pauline epistles mention a ministry in Crete. Some interpreters suggest that Paul was freed from the imprisonment in Rome described in the last chapter of Acts. He returned to Asia Minor and Greece, the scene of many of his former labors. At that time he visited Crete as well as the places mentioned in the letters to Timothy.

The Mission of Titus

1:1-16

The Salutation (1:1-4)

Paul did not identify himself in terms of social status, educational background, or personal accomplishments. His personal identity came from his relationship to God. He was the "servant of God" or, literally, "slave of God." The phrase also speaks of his sense of dignity and mission. He was God's representative in the world—a position of the highest honor, dignity, and responsibility.

Paul was also Christ's "apostle." The word means "one who is sent." When Paul called himself an apostle, he used the term in a special way. He classified himself among those earlier apostles, such as Peter, James, and John, who had been called and commissioned directly by the risen Lord.

The pastoral role was an important function of the apostolic ministry. The apostle's task was not completed when people were converted. Their "faith" was undeveloped and "their knowledge of the truth" was incomplete. Paul was responsible for helping "God's elect" in both these areas. "God's elect" identifies the church as the chosen ones. God's choice, his initiative in salvation, always precedes and makes possible the human response of faith.

"The truth" does not consist of abstract intellectual concepts. It is "truth which accords with godliness." In the Pastorals "godliness" means the Christian way of life. It has an extremely practical meaning. The emphasis is on truth as it is lived out in the world.

The goal of the apostolic ministry was the "hope of eternal life." Eternal life was assured because it had been "promised" by a faithful God who does not lie. The promise was given substance by its manifestation in history. The "word" is the message of God's redemptive deed in the death and resurrection of Jesus Christ. This is the message which Paul had proclaimed in obedience to the trust God had placed in him by calling him.

Titus, the recipient of the letter, was one of Paul's closest missionary associates. Paul called Titus his "true child." In common usage this meant natural, as opposed to an adopted or foster child. This father-son relationship, however, is understood in the context of the community of faith. Perhaps Paul had won Titus to Christ.

The greeting is the standard Pauline one. "Grace," God's unmerited love, is the basis of our relationship to him. "Peace" is the new relationship which we enjoy with God and his people because of his grace. We have been reconciled to God and to one another.

The Qualifications of Elders (1:5-9)

We find no reference in the other epistles or in Acts of Paul's visit to Crete or of Titus' ministry there (see Introduction). The apostle evidently felt it necessary to leave the island before finishing his work there. He had left Titus behind to finish the task. "What was defective" means "what was left unfinished."

One of the main unfinished tasks was the appointment of church leaders to stabilize churches which were the targets of pernicious, false teachings. These leaders are called "elders" (v. 5) or "bishops" (v. 7). First in importance in the letter is the quality of the elder's family life. He should be the "husband of one wife" (KJV) or "faithful to his one wife" (NEB).

The character of the prospective elder's children was also important. First, they were to be "believers." Clearly children were to exercise personal faith in the same way as their parents. Second, they should not be guilty of immoral living or of a rebellious attitude toward their father.

An ideal which should guide the church is stated in verse 6. The elder "must be blameless." In actual practice we always have to settle for less, since the people who are chosen are always imperfect. Nevertheless, we must keep the ideal before us. The importance of the bishop's (elder's) task is underlined in the phrase "God's steward." The steward, often a slave in ancient times, had responsibility for managing the master's household and property. The bishop is responsible for managing God's household, the church; and he is responsible to God. As God's steward he is to be thoroughly Christian in attitude and action.

This means that some things are to be avoided. He should "not be arrogant or quick-tempered or a drunkard or violent or greedy" for personal wealth. How many churches have been thrown into a crisis because a leader had one or more of these bad traits! Certain positive virtues characterize the good bishop. Hospitality was very important in those early days when it was necessary to entertain traveling Christians in the home. Goodness, uprightness, holiness, and self-control are qualities essential for church leadership.

The bishop functioned as the teacher of the church. It was essential, therefore, for him to be unswerving in his allegiance to the sure word as taught. An example of this sure word in Titus is found in 2:11-14. The bishop was responsible for instructing the flock. He also had the task of protecting it by refuting the false teachings of the people who would lead it astray.

Danger from False Teachers (1:10-16)

The problem confronting the churches in Crete was serious. They were being disrupted by false teachers. These were "many" in number, and their teachings were extremely dangerous. Paul described their character in especially harsh terms. They were "insubordinate," rebellious against the duly constituted leadership of the churches. They belonged to the "circumcision party." This was a sect of legalists who wanted to make certain practices, including circumcision, mandatory for membership in the church. Paul had a constant battle with legalists who wanted to impose circumcision on Gentile converts (see Gal. 2:1-10; Phil. 3:2 ff.).

The impact of the false teachers was considerable; they were "upsetting whole families." Paul felt that they were exploiting the churches for "base gain," for personal financial profit. Paul endorsed a description of Cretans attributed to one of their own. He characterized them as "liars, evil beasts," and "lazy gluttons." The apostle felt that the false teachers in the churches were still under the influence of the worst in Crete's moral climate. We note that he did not regard them as totally hopeless, however. Timothy was instructed to "rebuke them sharply," but the purpose of the rebuke was redemptive. Perhaps it would cause them to become "sound in the faith."

Two aspects of the false teaching are mentioned in verse 14. The first is speculative interpretations of Old Testament passages called "Jewish myths." The second is "commands," evidently legalistic requirements. They probably classified certain things as impure. People who ate or touched the forbidden things became unclean.

Paul rejected the classification of material things into categories of pure and impure. "To the pure all things are pure." The genuine believer can eat or touch anything without fear of being defiled. It is certainly true that we as Christians may decide not to eat or drink certain things. But this decision is not determined by religious taboos. We make our decision about diet in the light of scientific knowledge about what is helpful or harmful to the body.

"To the corrupt and unbelieving nothing is pure." No observance of distinctions between pure and impure things can change the unbeliever's heart and make it pure. The problem is not with the outside but with the inside of the individual. When people are not Christians, "their very minds and consciences are corrupted." They are defiled on the inside. Only the power of God can alter this situation by bringing about an inner transformation.

As we have had occasion to see in the Pastorals, Paul was concerned above all else with Christian living. There is an intimate, essential relationship between belief and behavior. Paul saw no such relationship in the lives of the false teachers. They professed "to know God" but denied him "by their deeds." This is not surprising, since they were known for their rebellion. People who are "disobedient" to God are simply "unfit for any good deed."

The Teaching Duties of the Minister
2:1-15

Instructions for Various Groups (2:1-10)

In contrast to the false teachers, Titus was admonished to teach that which was in keeping with "sound doctrine." We see from the instructions which follow how much sound doctrine is understood as practical teaching for Christian living.

The older men (2:2).—"Temperate, serious," and "sensible" are translated in various ways in different versions. This means that it is difficult to determine their precise meaning in English. Mastery of oneself is certainly one of the ideas prominent in these words. Excess is a danger to be avoided, whether it has to do with alcoholic beverages or with other appetites. The word "serious" refers to conduct which inspires respect. Older men are to be "sound" in three areas—"in faith, in love, and in steadfastness." Faith is trust in God, manifested in loyal Christian living. Love is that commitment to the welfare of other people without regard to their merit. Steadfastness is a triumphant stance in the face of persecution and difficulties. Faith toward God, love toward others, and steadfastness before the hostility of the world are the ingredients of the genuine Christian life.

The older women (2:3-5).—The older women are to be "reverent in behavior," conducting themselves as people who live their lives before God. This is interpreted negatively. They are not to be "slanderers." The inclination to engage in character assassination has always been a problem for churches. Furthermore, godly women are not to be "slaves to drink." This prohibition indicates that the abuse of alcohol was a problem in the early church. Today in an affluent society in which many people have a great deal of leisuretime, the problem is even more acute.

Older women were given a responsibility for a teaching ministry in the church. Their pupils were the "young women." Questions are raised about this passage in our modern society which were not even possible in earlier times. Women did not have opportunities for professional employment in the ancient world. Their main sphere of Christian opportunity and responsibility was the home. Paul wanted the older women to teach the younger ones to be good wives and mothers.

Note the basic reason for the counsel. The writer was anxious that the gospel "not be discredited." It was important to him that people not be turned away from the "word of God" by those who professed it.

The younger men (2:7-8).—The virtue of self-control, urged upon "younger men," was also a characteristic prescribed for the older ones (2:2). The adjective "sensible" in verse 2 is a cognate of the verb translated "to control themselves" here.

Possibly because he was nearer to them in age, Titus was to serve as an example to younger men. Once again the stress is put upon Christian living; he was to be "a model in good deeds." If the deeds of the Christian leader do not measure up to his words, his influence is undermined. Teaching characterized by "integrity" and "gravity" is also important. Integrity describes character that cannot be corrupted by the flattery of the false teachers. Gravity underlines the need to be serious, not flippant, in presenting truth.

In the Pastorals "sound speech" can refer to orthodox preaching. Perhaps here, however, the meaning is broader. Titus' life and teaching were watched by people who were antagonistic to the gospel.

He was to be so earnest and honest in what he said that those enemies would have no foundation for an attack. They would be frustrated, or "put to shame," in their efforts to discredit the gospel.

Instructions for slaves (2:9-10).—The institution of slavery is indefensible from the Christian point of view. Paul believed that the division between slave and free belonged to the old order that was under the judgment of God. In the church, which belonged to the new order, there was "neither slave nor free" (Gal. 3:28).

The church had no hope in the first century, however, of changing the pagan order through social reform. That would have to wait for an era when Christians were numerous enough to use their influence to help abolish a cruel, inhuman institution. Under the conditions of the ancient world, the only advice the apostle could give to believing slaves was to be Christian in their slavery. Their Christian character could be demonstrated through obedience, honesty, and faithfulness.

Note the motivation urged by the writer upon Christian slaves. They were to live in a way that would "adorn the doctrine of God our Savior." The NEB gives an interesting translation of 10*b*: "for in all such ways they will add lustre to the doctrine of God our Saviour." We often live in difficult circumstances that we cannot change. Nevertheless, we can use the difficult circumstances to glorify God and to cause other people to want him as their Savior.

The Christian Hope (2:11-15)

The Christian life is lived between two events. The first took place when the "grace of God . . . appeared." This refers to that crucial event, the incarnation, when the Word made flesh was born, lived, died, and was raised from the dead. What Christ did was the supreme expression of God's love for "all men." God's grace, therefore, is universal in scope. It transcends all human categories of race, sex, class, and culture.

We know that Jesus came into the world as the highest manifestation of God's grace. We also know that he will appear again in "glory." All our thoughts and actions are to be directed toward this expectation. For the believer to live a life of "irreligion," dominated by "worldly passions," is a contradiction. Jesus died to "redeem us from all iniquity." "Redeem" was often used to describe the process of freeing a slave from his bondage. In the New Testament it is used to describe the mighty, liberating act of God who frees us from slavery to sin.

Jesus also "gave himself . . . to purify for himself a people of his own." "People of his own" translates an interesting phrase taken from the Septuagint (Ex. 19:5; Deut. 14:2; Ezek. 37:23). The phrase describes the people which constitute "the crown jewel of God." Through Jesus' work of redemption God brought into being a people, who are his priceless possession. Immorality is inconsistent with this status conferred upon us by God. In view of this special relation with God, believers are to take their moral and ethical lives seriously. But purity is not only, or primarily, negative. We are to be "zealous for good deeds" or "eager to do good."

General Instructions for Christian Living

3:1-15

Christian Conduct in the World (3:1-7)

Relationship to rulers (3:1).—The believer's real king is God himself and not some pagan ruler. He belonged to God's people and possessed a heavenly citizenship. This evidently provoked certain questions in the early churches. Is God's servant to be subservient to a human authority? Is he to be concerned about the affairs of this world?

The writer took a positive attitude toward the government, as is also true of 1 Peter (2:13-14). The government was viewed as beneficent, a help rather than a hindrance to the gospel, when the Pastorals were written. According to this passage, the duty of the believer in civic matters is threefold. He is to be "submissive"—that is, recognize that he is a subject of the state. He is to obey the authorities. Also, he is to cooperate with them in "any honest work." Here the adjective "honest" (or honorable) qualifies work. It implies that the believer is not to do anything dishonorable.

In the book of Revelation another situation existed. The state is the enemy of the gospel; and the emperor is the beast, the tool of Satan. In those circumstances the Christian is called upon to die rather than obey the idolatrous demands of the state.

Treatment of non-Christians (3:2-7).—The question of how Christians were to relate to their pagan neighbors was especially difficult in those early days. Church members, a minority of the population in every place, were often objects of pagan and Jewish hostility and slander. According to Paul's instructions, the relations of believers to non-Christians were to be governed by the principles of love. Their conversation about or with their unbelieving contemporaries was not to be anything but loving, gentle, and courteous.

Certainly hostile people whose moral and ethical conduct was far below Christian norms gave many occasions for resentment. But the writer reminded the churches through Titus that they were once just like their neighbors. They also had been "foolish." In Scripture the foolish person does not know God and does not understand his truths. The wise person is open to the insight of God's truth. The church members had been "disobedient" to God and had been "led astray," victims of evil's deception. Their moral lives had been low. Their relationships to their fellowmen had been characterized by "malice and envy." The passage presents an altogether unlovely description of the base existence of many pagans in Crete.

Paul knew that self-righteousness was always a danger to Christians who had emerged from the low condition of paganism. They could take credit for their new moral and religious superiority. The writer, therefore, reminded the Christians of Crete that their new situation before God was not due to any merit of their own. As he said, the believers' salvation was not the result of deeds done by us. It was rooted solely in the "goodness and loving kindness of God." Generally, the love of God is expressed by the Greek word *agape*. Here a less forceful word is used. It is the word from which we derive our term philanthropy. The NEB translates it "generosity."

Verses 4-7 compose one of the great statements of the New Testament on the meaning of salvation. Various perspectives on the saving act of God and what it means are emphasized. The verb "saved" underlines the fact that it is a deliverance. Sinners are under the evil power of sin. They are its victims. Their future is filled with threats. From all this God delivered them.

Paul also called it a "washing of regeneration." The word "regeneration" focuses on the meaning of salvation as a new birth. No doubt the writer was thinking about baptism, which was the public expression of a decision for Christ in the early church. But it is not the water that saves. It is God's power which brings life to the person who decides for him through faith in Christ. The believer also experiences "renewal in the Holy Spirit." This passage agrees with the consistent teaching of the New Testament. The gift of the Spirit is connected with the beginning of the Christian life. At the moment of belief the sinner is renewed by the Holy Spirit.

There is another important point. The renewing power of the Spirit comes to the Christian "through Jesus Christ our Savior." To separate the gift of the Holy Spirit from the moment of conversion does an injustice to New Testament theology. To make our relationship to Jesus Christ and our relationship to the Holy Spirit something separate and distinct is also an error.

Conversion means at least this. The Father sends the Spirit through Jesus Christ to those who accept his Son as Savior and brings into being a new creature. "Justified by his grace" is a typically Pauline way of talking about the conversion experience. "Justified" is basically a legal term. It describes the act of the judge who acquits or exonerates the accused person. However, we as sinners are not justified, or acquitted, by God because of our innocence. We are "justified by his grace"— that is, his unmerited favor and love which go out to us even though we are guilty.

Finally, our new nature as regenerated or "born again ones" and our new relationship to God as justified ones make it possible for us to have the confident "hope of eternal life." When we are regenerated, we become children of God and, therefore, his "heirs." What we shall inherit is the life of glory. This, of course, still lies in the future. Like any other heir who has not received his full inheritance, our attitude now is one of "hope" or expectancy. But this hope is not wishful thinking. It arises out of our knowledge of the kind of Father we have.

Dealing with Factious Persons (3:8-11)

The sure saying of verse 8 refers to what Paul wrote about the believer's salvation. This kind of statement is at the very center of the Christian gospel and doctrine. It is the kind of thing that Titus is to "insist on." In response to the God who has acted in such a marvelous way to redeem sinners, there will come the "good deeds" of the redeemed person's life. The kinds of things Paul was interested in would be "useful to their fellow-men" (NEB).

Another religious system in Crete was vying for acceptance alongside that defended in this epistle. Once again a hint about the nature of the heresy shines through the description of our text. One of its major problems was its speculative nature, which consequently pro-

voked "dissensions." Evidently fanciful interpretations of the genealogical passages of the Old Testament were involved. The false teachers found hidden spiritual meanings in them.

There were also "dissensions and quarrels over the law." We may
assume that the Jewish law of the Old Testament is meant here. We
may also assume that the false teachers argued over how it was to
be applied to the Christian life. Probably they held to some kind of
legalism which made the keeping of the law, as they interpreted it,
essential to Christian living. Arguments over theological speculations
are "unprofitable and futile." Faithfulness to the gospel produces a
united community of love. By contrast, theological speculations divide
the body of Christ.

How was the church to deal with the "factious" person? He was
to be admonished "once or twice" in an effort to get him to forsake
his divisive activities. If he persisted in his course of action, however,
the church was to sever relations with him. "Is perverted" is past
tense, while "sinful" is in the present tense in Greek. Perhaps that
tense should be translated here so as to bring out its central emphasis
on continuous action. The idea would then be: "he has been perverted
and persists in his sinful way." Persistence in sin and refusal to change
indicate that the person who adheres to the false teaching has put
himself outside the fellowship. "He is self-condemned." He refuses
to heed the counsel of those who are trying to win him from his
erring ways. This refusal is in essence his own condemnation of himself.

Closing Remarks (3:12-15)

When either Artemas or Tychicus was sent to Crete, Titus was to
make an effort to rejoin Paul. Artemas is not mentioned elsewhere.
Tychicus was the bearer of the epistle to the Colossians (Col. 4:7;
see also Acts 20:4). Paul planned to send one of them to take the
place of Titus so that he would be free to leave his responsibility in
their hands.

Paul planned to spend the winter in "Nicopolis," a common name
of the period. We do not know which Nicopolis is meant. Once again
the autobiographical notes given here do not fit into anything we
know of Paul's life from other sources.

We know nothing of Zenas. Appolos was probably the gifted
preacher from Alexandria who labored in Ephesus and Corinth. Titus
and the Christians in Crete are to "speed Zenas . . . and Appolos
on their way." This had become a technical expression for providing

for the material needs of traveling missionaries as they departed so that they would not suffer from lack of food on their journey. This is brought out by Paul's admonition: "See that they lack nothing." Verse 14 may be connected with the preceding. If the urgent needs of the traveling preachers were to be met, it would be done through the "good deeds" of the Christians in Crete.

The close of the letter was in keeping with the practice of letter writing of the day. The final greeting is typically Pauline. From his point of view, the Christian life was a matter of grace from beginning to end. We are saved by grace, sustained by grace, and enter into our inheritance by grace. Paul could ask no higher blessing on Titus and his charges than that they continue to receive the grace of God.

PHILEMON

Introduction

This beautiful and touching letter was written by the apostle Paul on behalf of Onesimus, a runaway slave. Paul was a prisoner when he wrote the letter. Customarily interpreters have assumed that this was the Roman imprisonment mentioned in Acts. Caesarea and Ephesus have been suggested, however, as other possibilities.

After escaping from his master, Onesimus had come into contact with the imprisoned apostle. Subsequently Paul decided that he should return to his master and wrote this brief letter to be delivered to him at the slave's arrival.

In a letter written in the early second century, Ignatius of Antioch mentioned an Onesimus who was the bishop of Ephesus. The supposition that Onesimus the slave and Onesimus the bishop were the same person is very attractive. If this is true, Philemon may have decided to free his slave in response to Paul's letter. Onesimus then showed himself to be worthy of the love and trust of Paul and Philemon by rising to a place of leadership in the church.

Philemon and Colossians were evidently written and dispatched at the same time. The same persons sent greetings in both letters (see Col. 4:10-14 and Philem. 23-24). Onesimus is also mentioned in Colossians 4:9. A few scholars have argued that Philemon is the letter to the neighboring church in Laodicea mentioned in Colossians 4:16. If this is not the case, Philemon was sent to Colossae, for Paul described Onesimus as "one of yourselves" (Col. 4:9).

The Salutation (1-3)

Above all, in this letter Paul did not want to take an authoritative stance. Therefore, he did not describe himself as an apostle, one who had the right to command. This letter is a warm, poignant plea to Philemon on behalf of the slave Onesimus. Force was added to that plea when Paul stressed that it came from one who knew what suffering and sacrifice were. He was "a prisoner," but the meaning of his imprisonment is described in the phrase "for Christ Jesus." He had

164

been captured by the Lord long ago. Because of his service to Christ, the apostle was suffering imprisonment. Timothy was at his imprisoned friend's side when Paul wrote this letter.

The letter is addressed to three people and a congregation. Usually interpreters believe that Philemon was the slave owner. We do not know why Apphia and Archippus were mentioned. All three may have belonged to the same family. Or Archippus may have been a minister of the church that met in Philemon's house. "Church" could describe all the believers in a city, or a smaller group which met in a place, such as a home. Although Philemon is the most personal of Paul's letters, it is also addressed to the church. Paul's plea to Philemon and his friend's response were matters of concern to the whole group. In Paul's theology the Christian always acts as a member of the redeemed community and in the context of his relationship.

Paul's Prayer for Philemon (4-7)

As is common in Paul's letters, a prayer for the recipient follows the greeting. The prayer follows his customary pattern of thanksgiving and intercession.

The two primary aspects of the Christian life, "faith" and "love," are the causes of Paul's gratitude to God. We do not know exactly how verse 5 should be interpreted. Are faith and love directed toward "the Lord Jesus and all the saints"? In this case, faith would be understood as faithfulness or loyalty. But Jesus may be the object of faith and the saints the recipients of Philemon's love. Faith would have the meaning of trust in this interpretation. "Saints" is one of Paul's words for all God's people, both weak and strong, both erring and righteous. Philemon understood that no believers should be excluded from the circle of his love.

Verses 6-7 are very obscure, as you can see by comparing various translations. Perhaps the best we can do is to attempt to see the major ideas in Paul's prayer for Philemon. Paul believed that the Christian lived in a community of faith and that he was to participate actively in that community through his own life of trust in Jesus Christ. He believed that such a life would be characterized by active support, encouragement, and generosity toward the less fortunate. When a believer actively shared in the fellowship in that way, the result was a greater "knowledge of all the good that is ours in Christ." We do not know if he was praying for an increase of Philemon's knowledge of the blessings bestowed on the church by its Lord. It may be that

Paul saw the church gaining a greater knowledge of the blessings of its fellowship through Philemon's good and generous activity.

Paul did refer specifically to the influence of Philemon in the church. He had "refreshed" the "hearts of the saints"—or, as the TEV phrases it, he had "cheered the hearts of all God's people." In turn this had also brought "joy and comfort" to the imprisoned apostle. Probably Paul referred to Philemon's generous acts of love toward other believers because he was about to address an important appeal to his friend. He wanted Philemon to do yet another loving act which would inspire his brothers.

An Appeal to Love (8-14)

Paul knew that he had the authority "in Christ" to command Philemon. He probably also believed that Philemon would obey an apostolic injunction because he also recognized that authority. Philemon believed that Christ had called Paul to be an an apostle and that his words were to be heeded by other believers.

But Paul spurned the way of command. He preferred to appeal to the love of which Philemon had given such clear evidence. Three people were intensely and personally involved in the transaction Paul had in mind. Paul, Onesimus, and Philemon all had a stake in it. Paul wanted all three, not just Onesimus and himself, to benefit from any decision made. Thus he had to give Philemon an opportunity to act according to his faith and love. He would not deprive his friend of the privilege of doing a genuinely Christian deed.

Paul emphasized that the appeal came from him personally. "Ambassador" may also be translated "old man." This certainly adds a poignant note. Philemon is receiving a heartfelt plea from an old man who is also a prisoner. However, "ambassador" also makes sense. The ambassador for Christ became a prisoner as a result of representing him in a hostile world.

Only in verse 10 does the motive for Paul's letter become apparent. He is making an appeal for Onesimus, a slave belonging to Philemon. But this is not just a preacher speaking for a convert. This is a "father" pleading for his "child." Onesimus had trusted Christ through the witness of the imprisoned apostle.

"Useless" and "useful" involve a play on words in Greek not apparent in English. Both are compound words containing a word which sounded exactly like *Christos* (Christ). What had made such a difference in Onesimus' life? Christ had brought about the transformation, changing him from a useless to a useful person.

Paul desired to keep Onesimus with him. Indeed, he could have justified it as a service rendered to him by his friend in his imprisonment. But to do so would have been wrong, for it would have taken the decision out of Philemon's hand. Christians are to do good by their "own free" will and "not by compulsion." But Paul stressed how difficult the decision was. It was like sending his "very heart" (v. 12). It was as though Paul himself stood before Philemon in the person of the slave.

The Conclusion of the Appeal (15-20)

We must assume that Onesimus had run away from Philemon. There is a great deal about the whole episode we would like to know. Why had Philemon not won Onesimus to Christ? Perhaps his influence bore fruit later on when his slave came to know Paul. At any rate, Paul suggested in verse 15 that the providence of God was at work in the whole affair. If Onesimus had not run away, he might not have become a believer. Because he was a Christian, however, the temporary relationship between the slave and his owner had become eternal. They would inherit the kingdom together. As a slave, Philemon possessed Onesimus only in this life; as a "brother," he belonged to him "for ever." "In the flesh and in the Lord" may mean "as man and as a Christian" (NEB).

"Partner" translates one of Paul's favorite words for describing the relationship among Christians. They share together the mutual life in Christ, both in terms of its benefits and its responsibilities. Paul and Philemon were partners in the greatest of all enterprises. Paul had stressed this partnership in the address when he called Philemon a "fellow worker" (v. 1). On the basis of this relationship, he asked Philemon to receive his slave as he would receive his long-time partner in the gospel.

The apostle went even further. If Philemon had suffered any loss, he was not to look to Onesimus for repayment. Paul himself would stand good for any debt incurred as a result of the slave's escape. We have no way of knowing how Paul meant to repay such a debt. Indeed, he quickly reminded Philemon of his own debt. Philemon owed his "own self" to Paul. This may indicate that Paul had also been instrumental in winning Philemon to Christ. At any rate, it is clear that Philemon owed more to Paul than Onesimus could possibly owe to his owner.

What did Paul mean when he wrote: "I want some benefit from you in the Lord"? Did he mean that he only wanted Philemon to receive Onesimus as a Christian brother? Or was there something more at stake? The verb "want some benefit" is very close in sound to Onesimus. Perhaps he wanted Philemon to understand that the desired benefit was the return of Onesimus to him. The whole letter may be understood as a very delicate request for Philemon to free his slave so that he might rejoin the apostle. Because he did not want to use compulsion, the apostle thoughtfully refrained from making his request in a direct fashion.

Philemon had refreshed the hearts of the saints (v. 7). Now Paul made the request that his friend do the same for him: "refresh my heart in Christ." Nothing would have cheered him more than to have his beloved child once more at his side.

Final Remarks (21-25)

Love and confidence are much more effective in calling forth the best in other people than are hostility and suspicion. We generally strive to fulfill the expectations of those we love. Paul understood that and reinforced his appeal to Philemon by an affirmation of confidence in him. He expected his friend to go beyond what he was asked to do in the letter. If Philemon merited this confidence at all, Paul did not have to spell out clearly what he should do. Love always goes far beyond duty.

Paul was in prison, but he was evidently optimistic about the future. He believed he would be freed and planned to return to the area of his former ministry to visit the churches. Believers normally provided food and lodging for traveling evangelists like Paul. The request for a "guest room" was very normal under the circumstances.

Several of Paul's associates joined him in the final greeting. Epaphras was the evangelist who had first preached the gospel in Colossae (Col. 1:7). Mark, Aristarchus, Demas, and Luke are also mentioned at the conclusion of Colossians, probably written and dispatched at the same time (see Col. 4:10-14).

Paul normally ended his letters with a prayer for the greatest blessing of all for his recipients. That blessing is "grace," God's love which is poured out continually upon his people. In the phrase "your spirit," "your" is plural, indicating that Paul's request was that God's grace be given to the whole church.